THE TOP

UNIVERSAL TOY, ENDURING PASTIME

THE TOP

UNIVERSAL TOY, ENDURING PASTIME

D. W. GOULD

Clarkson N. Potter, Inc./Publisher NEW YORK

DISTRIBUTED BY CROWN PUBLISHERS, INC.

Printed in the United States of America
Library of Congress Catalog Card Number: 79-169050
ISBN: 0-517-504162
Published simultaneously in Canada by General Publishing
Company Limited.
Inquiries should be addressed to Clarkson N. Potter, Inc.
419 Park Avenue South, New York, N.Y. 10016.
Designed by Shari de Miskey
FIRST EDITION

*Over 100 original line drawings by
Jo McMahon with additional illustrations
by Deborah Daly*

ACKNOWLEDGMENTS

I HAVE drawn heavily from the resources of the Museum of the University of Pennsylvania in Philadelphia. The nucleus of their collection of tops dates to the efforts of S. Culin around the beginning of this century, and has been augmented by archaeologists and anthropologists. But it is the long list of library workers responding to obscure or seemingly unrelated requests who have borne the brunt. Particularly is this true in Metropolitan Philadelphia. To the late Dr. J. Walter Wilson of Brown University for his encouragement and cordial access to his collection of tops, my thanks. And to Dr. Miller of Haverford College for his constructive guidance in setting forth a non-mathematical explanation of the top's behavior, my appreciation.

CONTENTS

PREFACE

Play is a necessity of life for children, youth and grown-ups. For it is one of the primary forms of mingling with the world about. Therefore give to others the opportunity for play, and don't neglect to play, yourself.

Play is purposeless, yet it can be made to bring together all possible purposes. The experience of an unrestrained yet legitimate act of play outweighs the educational goals which man substitutes for play. Down with play which has worthwhile, reasonable considerations!

Play as a counterweight to work is not only a means of preserving health, but it is also a necessity for a life which does not wear itself out in the sole pursuit of requirements. Without play, there is no complete life for man.

H. HETZER, 1935

THIS BOOK came to be written and was sustained by a very accidental turn of affairs. A visit to a toy store to buy a top for a boy of prime top-spinning age was marked by the proprietor's ". . . but we shall probably have some in the top-spinning season," and there was offered an enormous metallic humming-top that only an adult could operate.

That same year I was to witness the superb adult top-play of Malaysia. Somehow I felt that this remote society had retained an enjoyment that was on the verge of extinction in America, and that if the hands of time could not be stopped, there should be at least a clearer record of what had been.

When debating what material should appear in the text, many questions arose, such as, "What is a top?" or "When is a toy a top?" Some were never completely answered. In the interests of writing a general text, many technicalities had to be omitted. This study will treat the top almost wholly as a toy. Although developments in the gyroscope will be pointed out, the technological application of the top as a gyroscope is adequately treated elsewhere. And, while it is true that the top is used as an adult gambling device (equivalent, say, to the six-faced die), it is such a minor part of its use that we shall not deal with it here. The spiritual implications of the top, on the other hand, will be discussed.

It was necessary to classify tops and to assign names to these classes. Although some names previously used were found inadequate or downright inapplicable, they are sometimes retained. For example, pegs are not necessary to peg-tops; they provide a contact surface that resists wear and have been used to advantage on whip-tops as well. I have used the name peg-top to describe a type of top which is cast by the user even though the years have slowly eroded that meaning of the verb form PEG: to throw. And humming-tops do not always hum: when any top gives out a pleasing sound, perhaps it should be called a hummer. The reader will discover other inconsistencies.

BIBLIOGRAPHY — AN ANTICIPATION

Although it appears at the end of the book, the bibliography is intended as an integral part of it, to be used throughout. An understanding of its structure will help. There are only a few direct citations in the main text, and these are referred to by the author's name and number of bibliographical entry rather than by footnotes. Following each chapter there may be numbers listed that correspond to bibliographical entries. The substance of the several articles represented by the numbers is to be considered the factual basis of the text. The reader can sometimes make his own assessment of original authorship by taking into account the medium (journal, book, etc.) in which the subject matter appears. Thus, the archaeologist or the physicist reporting in his professional media might be given more weight than the general traveler writing for magazine readers. A few exceptions, however, can nullify confidence in such a course, and one reluctantly concludes that top-spinning, although one of man's oldest leisure activities, has left no clear record in the millennia, nor is it likely that exact reconstruction from the scanty data available will be made.

BIBLIOGRAPHICAL REFERENCES

13, 62, 63, 73, 136, 141, 172, 176, 193, 198, 207, 218, 252

THE
TOP

UNIVERSAL TOY, ENDURING PASTIME

INTRODUCTION

WHAT IT'S ALL ABOUT

MAN HAS always been fascinated by the top. He regards it with wonder because it is an object to which he can impart controlled motion. The motion is both visible and nearby, as opposed to a ball or projected object that quickly comes to rest and at a distance. For a brief instant man is a god and has seized a bit of magic; he has made an object stand erect in defiance of gravity. Webster's Dictionary defines the top as "a child's toy having a tapering, usually steel-shod point on which it is made to spin" (Figure 1).

◄
Figure 1. Common top.

A D U L T   A S P E C T S   O F   T H E   M A T T E R

We might infer from Webster and general consensus that the top is only part of a child's world, whereas in fact, throughout history, the top has fascinated all ages. The intrusion of adults into this child's world has come about through their participation in the activity and the necessity to use their skills and tools to fashion any but the simplest of tops.

In primitive societies, such as Malay, top-spinning attained the status of an organized adult sport and this has persisted into modern times. The element of play shares with the spirit of competition. The equipment is often professionally made and children of both sexes are excluded from the contests. Women do not participate; their presence and that of the children is neither sought nor prohibited. Haddon [178]* wrote that the natives of Mer (Torres Strait) played so assiduously at top-spinning as to neglect their gardens, and the sport had to be constrained. And, in Borneo and Java, the size, weight, and workmanship of their tops preclude any but adult use. Again, Haddon describes the care bestowed on this property. It seems that special baskets were made solely to carry tops. Reed and others indicate that the Pacific Islanders gave a spiritual meaning to the top and it was often hung on a man's grave (although some cultures allowed a close relative to remove it). Further, it is said that the hum of a top gave solace to the defeated warrior.

In medieval times, there was the parish top, literally the communal top for everybody's use, and the users were adults.

In the Orient, throughout history, the public entertainers, such as the jugglers and top-spinners, were adult professionals. It was expected that the required skill could be attained only by adults.†

---

* Numbers refer to bibliographical entries.

† Not wholly valid. Joya speaks of a boy in the 1700s who was a professional and astonished the spectators with his skill. The account is clouded by inclusion of a statement to the effect that the top could be spun for several hours; acceptable only as a bit of legerdemain.

As far as modern societies are concerned, America has had adult top-spinners of notable ability, among them a trio of Chicagoans who developed peg-top spinning to a high degree of skill just for the fun of it. And, in France, there was a time not too long ago when adult Frenchmen joined an organization called Société des Amateurs des Jouets et des Jeux Anciennes where they played with toys, including tops.*

Of course, a study of the top can be justified merely on the basis of the top's successful application (in the form of the gyroscope) to the social, industrial and martial affairs of today. But even less sophisticated tops are used with an artistry that goes beyond a mere pastime and bespeaks a concentrated and persistent will to surpass in performance—this alone takes the top beyond a child's world. For myself, I must admit to a selfish absorption with the top and the sheer delight of mastering a difficult physical exercise.

* The organization is believed to have been a casualty of World War I.

CHAPTER ONE

HISTORY

ALTHOUGH LITERATURE on tops is scarce, the top is often mentioned in classical literature. For example, in Aristophanes' *The Birds* (1461)

> *(Informer):* "You get the idea. I'm busy as a top."
> *(Pisthetairos* takes a long whiplash): "Top? Here's something to make tops spin."

and Homer in the *Iliad* (XIV. 413): ". . . reels like a top staggering to its last turnings." Plato uses technical terms in the *Republic* (IV. 436, commentary): "A wheel or top which moves upon a fixed axis or center may be said to move or not to move, i.e., it may move at its circumference, while its axis (conceived as a vertical straight line) stands still." Further, Virgil in the *Aeneid* (VII. 378) says:

> *She wanders aimless, fevered and unstrung*
> *Along the public ways; as oft one sees*
> *Beneath the twisted whips a leaping top*

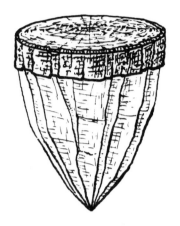
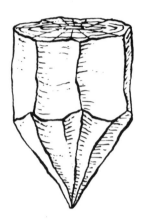
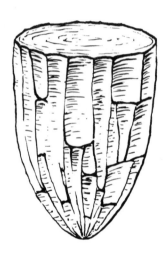
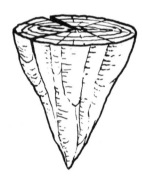
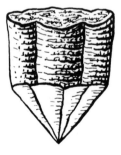

Sped in long spirals through a palace-close
By lads at play: obedient to the thong,
It weaves wide circles in the gaping view
Of its small masters, who admiring see
The whirling boxwood made a living thing
Under their lash.

Basil (St. Basilius) in *Hexamer* 5:

Like tops which, as a consequence of an initial impulse,
orient themselves and spin on their axes; so thus the order
of nature finds its first principle in this first law and then
goes through the entire sequence until it achieves comple-
tion of the system.

In none of these writings is there any light shed on the origin of the top; the technical aspects of the toy are inadequately treated. We must depend on art and archaeology, but the surviving representations of tops are so few as to raise the question whether the examples are typical. How much realism did the artist impart? How correct are the proportions of top to human? Artistic freedom was accepted then as now. Considering the trivial nature of the top, it is surprising to find it both a subject in art and an object of interest to the archaeologist.

There is hardly any indication in the oldest civilizations that tops were a part of the culture. There are a few specimens from Egypt (Figure 2) wholly of the whip-top variety, and one looks in vain for paintings or papyruses to describe the toy's use. Did Egypt's geographical location insulate it from exposure to other forms of the top, or has the topic merely been ignored in most Egyptologists' reports?

◄

Figure 2. Whip-tops. Egyptian, from 12th–18th dynasties, 2000–1400 B.C. (based on Petrie).

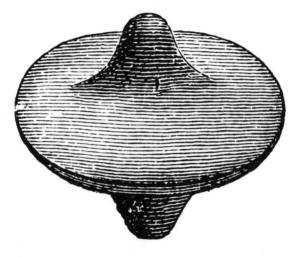

Figure 3. Ceramic spinner from Troy (based on Schliemann).

Schliemann's crude methods of excavation used a century ago would appall archaeologists today. Material remains were often destroyed or displaced. Most modern writers do not agree with Schliemann's assignment of level to Homeric Troy, but he did give a bold, reasoned interpretation of his discoveries. With the hindsight of a hundred years of experience in excavation of this site and others, we believe his interpretation wrong. We cannot gainsay his faith and brilliant work in selecting the site. The thousands of objects recovered by Schliemann are in great part terra-cotta (Figure 3). Metal, stone, and glass are far less in number. Wood, leather, cloth could not be expected to withstand deterioration by fire and weather.

Luckily, some lively examples of tops and top-spinning survive in Greek pottery. The line drawings we show here are but poor shadows of the ceramic originals. To compensate in part, a liberal number of bibliographical citations is given so that those interested may find adequate descriptions of these archaeological treasures. As for the literature of their place in common life, the treatment by Hoorn [202] and others is excellent.

Whip-tops and spinning are pictured in Figure 4 (b) and in Figures 5, 6, and 7. The scenes of women are particularly notable. The meaning of the action in Figure 5 (e), where the players are dispersed, is conjectural. Perhaps the human top-spinners have offended Olympians by playing with the latter's property. The winged figure may be the agent of the gods. It would seem that some of the tops were several inches in height; is this artistic license? There are no actual specimens of tops having the apparent dimensions of those pictured.

The ceramic models in Figure 7 (b) and (c) are believed to be votive, that is, offered at some shrine in gratitude for or requesting some divine favor. Figure 8 shows a yo-yo player and Figure 58 shows decorated ceramic discs that seem to indicate an accurate knowledge of the toy. That the material is ceramic may be a sign of affluence. Its use is fortunate, for if made of more perishable material the top would not have survived.

This is good exercife, and
we know no reafon why girls
fhould not ufe it, in modera-
tion, as well as boys; for, when
they have been working with
a needle for fome time in
cold weather, the exercife will
tend much to promote their
health.

a

Figure 4. Public opinion two millennia apart. (a) based on
Tuer; (b) based on Richter, Metropolitan Museum of
Art.

b

a

b

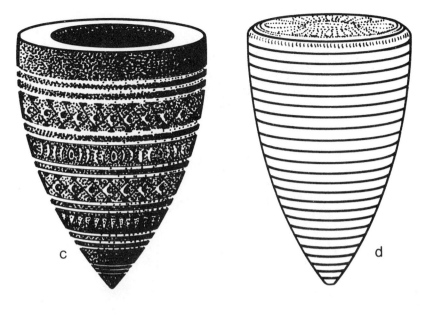

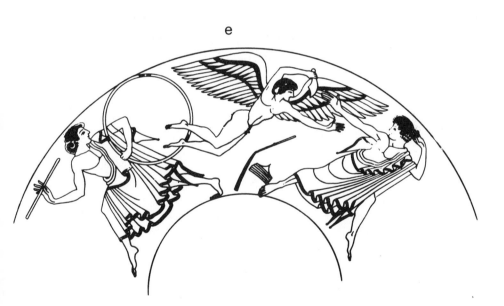

Figure 5. Classical whip-tops. (a) Hartwig; (b) Watzinger;
(c) British Museum; (d) Wolters; (e) Daremberg.

Figure 6. Three views of a classical Greek ceramic piece decorated to show whip-top spun by female (based on Froehner).

14

a

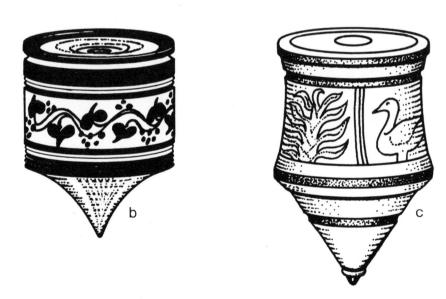

b

c

Figure 7. Classical whip-tops. (a) decoration (based on Langlotz); (b, c,) ceramic items that may be votive (based on Wolters and Boston Museum of Fine Arts).

15

Figure 8. Yo-yo. Vase adornment dated to about 500 B.C. (based on Benndorf).

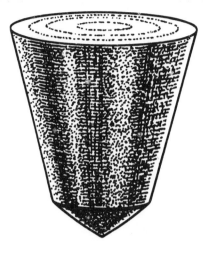

Figure 9. Terra-cotta whip-top dating to Roman occupation of Britain (based on Cuming).

The diffusion of the twirler throughout Europe as the Roman *teetotum* is certain. The whip-top may also owe its wide distribution to the Roman legions (see Figure 9 dating to the Roman occupation of Britain). There is conspicuous absence of the supported top; so far there is no clear evidence that it was known to the ancients, but possibly it is mere chance that none has survived.

In more recent times there is a remarkable number of scenes depicting top-spinning by children. The frequency suggests that the top was one of the favorite toys of the eighteenth and nineteenth centuries. The artists' efforts invariably show a skill in top-spinning never quite approached by this author at least. The

17

dimensions and shapes of the toys are usually credible (see Figure 10 as representative). Despite its antiquity, the top seems to have waited until the eighteenth century before it was dignified by mention in a title; a candidate for seniority might be Short's "An Account of an Horizontal Top; Invented by Mr. Serson," 1752. Smith's "Note on the Theory of the Spinning Top," 1846,[312] deserves mention because it was the forerunner in the new age of scientific invention. Woodbridge may have obtained the first United States patent on a top in the year 1854 (No. 11187, *Improvement in Whistling Tops*).

POSSIBLE ORIGINS OF THE TOP

Speculation upon the origin of the top is satisfying: the proponent of any theory can be challenged, but some part of his evidence can be convincingly demonstrable in some faraway culture. However, it seems necessary to stress that the top was observed before it was invented. Emerging homo sapiens would have noted and been amused, if not puzzled, by the falling maple seed (Figure 11). The spiraling of this seed can be repeated at will by any child tossing the seed into the air. The rotary motion of its fall, rather than the familiar oscillating descent of most leaves, is impressive and almost unique in the vegetable kingdom. But even if this natural phenomenon was denied early man because of geographical location, he could hardly have escaped bestowing passing attention on more durable objects—some of his own creation.

Harold Crabtree has discussed the rocking-oscillatory motion of certain Stone Age celts (shaped stones used as axes or chisels). If one gives a sharp downward tap on one end of the celt there results a strong rocking motion, and this oscillation gradually passes into a rotating motion. Another celt specimen, when given a brisk rotary motion, gradually slows, but as it ceases to

Figure 10. Children of tender age with whip-top and whip
in foreground (based on Allemagne).

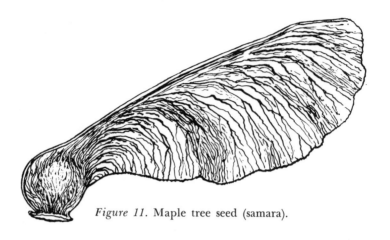

Figure 11. Maple tree seed (samara).

rotate takes on a decided, almost vigorous, rocking motion. We have repeated such experiments with museum specimens (Figure 12). The reader who does not have access to Stone Age celts can yet make a trial of the principle by rocking large clam shells upon a hard, smooth surface. One will note the astonishing decay of vibratory motion to a smooth rotary one. Trivial? Yes, but curiosity, observation, and invention often go together. The shape of early man's celts could have found counterparts in bone, ivory, and wood.

Whoever has thrown a stone platelet or a piece of slate (its lineal descendants are the Australian's boomerang and the college man's Frisbee) edge-on to the direction of flight has noted the probable arc to the left for a right-handed thrower, and a reverse direction for the left-handed person. The unconsciously administered spin imparted by the fingers makes a great difference between the flight of an object tossed, thrown, or projected (this latter is the action of the shot-putter).

The fire-drill is an invention of early man, used to create fire, and for those unfamiliar with such objects we show one form

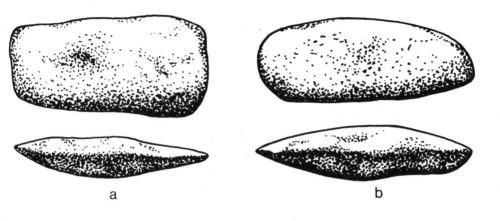

a

b

c

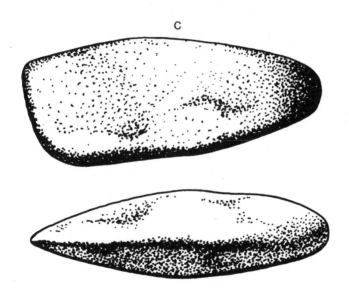

Figure 12. Celts exhibiting rocking-rotational motion. (a, b) eastern U.S.; (c) Lake Bienne, Switzerland. (Objects from University of Pennsylvania Museum.)

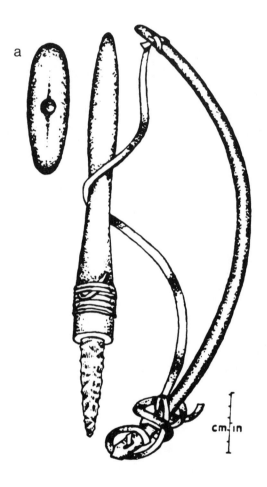

Figure 13. Fire-drill and bow. Object (a) is slipped over shaft and held by the fire-maker with left hand while the bow is manipulated by the right hand.

(Figure 13). The use of an added weight upon the shaft itself was a remarkable modification of the assembled tool. It imposed a considerable and uniform pressure at the friction point, something not readily done by an operator's left hand which must hold the shaft in a vertical position. The fire-drill's user, by moving the bow with alternate thrust and pull motions, gives a rapid rotary motion to the shaft and friction point. (The child imitating his elder would not stress the imposition of the added weight but would be happy to achieve the successive thrust and pull motions in a smooth manner.)

The transition from alternately clockwise and counterclockwise rotation (supposing the bowstring to be kept in tension) to a unidirectional motion was a notable discovery in itself. This transition can be brought about by relaxing the bowstring's tension on the shaft during one of the arm's lateral motions (pushing or pulling the bow). With this discovery was born the principle of the simple lathe, still in use today by craftsmen.

Travelers in the Eastern Hemisphere who have seen the woodworker seated on the ground before his lathe, guiding the chisel with his left hand and the toes of one foot, while alternately stroking the bow with his right hand to engage and relax on the turning shaft, have witnessed a scene of wonderful coordination of mind and muscle. (This writer, after many trials, succeeded in imparting unidirectional motion of the spindle, but got no further.)

We have intimated that the fire-drill could have led to the invention of a top, for there is a remote physical kinship between the drill and the tops which are classed as buzzers and supported-in-starting tops. Surveys of primitive cultures do not change the picture; the presence of tops is almost universal and the methods of making fire are many. With the advantage of hindsight, it is possible to see a relationship between the fire-drill, the twirler rotated by the palms of the hands (Figure 14), and the humming-top.

A case has also been made for the whorl, used in spinning fiber, as the forerunner of the top. Whorls (Figure 15) give

23

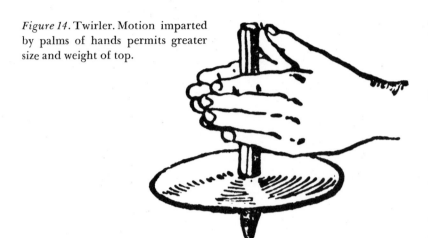

Figure 14. Twirler. Motion imparted by palms of hands permits greater size and weight of top.

tension and momentum of motion to the gathering and orderly stranding of the fibers. They have been found by archaeologists in scores of sites. The whorl (b) is conventional in shape and may be considered a rounded disc set on a shaft. Whorl (a) is typical of many found by Schliemann at Troy. The insertion of a short tapered piece of wood might convert these bits of ceramic into a twirler that a child could readily spin. The whorls found by Uhle in a pre-Columbian site in Peru (Figure 15c) have the same general shape as some present-day Japanese tops (Figure 104, items 29, 35). In the actual use of the whorl in (a) there might be derived the "buzzer" (class 5). Once discovered, the principle of placing the cord in tension would be embodied in the available materials of the day: fibers, tendons, strips of hide. It may be disputed whether the buzzer is a top, but it does have important affinities.

▶

Figure 15. Whorls. (a) ceramic whorl from Troy (based on Schliemann); (b) spindle and whorl (adapted from *Encyclopaedia Britannica*); (c) wooden whorls, pre-Columbian type from Cuzco, South America (based on Uhle).

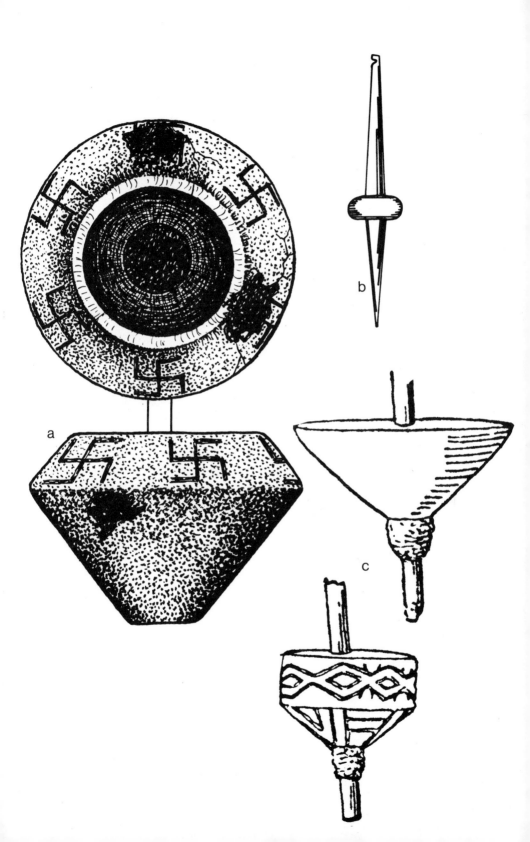

a

b

c

The earliest conventional tops were probably made of perishable materials and thus their survival would be wholly fortuitous. Most specimens from early history are ceramic and are perhaps votive rather than practical. Stone tops more recently found in primitive cultures are not considered prototypes, but rather exemplify the use of a material for the sake of durability and perhaps weight.

The potter's wheel also has its advocates as the forerunner of the top; one writer has noted that tops are found in all civilizations that have pottery. We shall anticipate our story a bit by showing (Figure 16) a potter's wheel bearing from Jericho and a Malayan top of the twentieth century. The similarity is accidental and no derivation of the top from the bearing is implied. Tops of the shape of the Malayan specimen have been found in cultures that did not have the potter's wheel.

Although anthropologists have found tops associated with surviving Stone Age cultures, there is no evidence that these cultures received the toy by diffusion in recent millennia. It is more logical to assume that the top has long been known, having been invented and re-invented by different cultures independently of one another.

Walter Kaudern, who collected many specimens of tops in the Celebes, observed no whip-tops, but twirlers and peg-tops were everywhere. He offered the interesting comparison of a sling-stone (a very old device used as a weapon) and the cord-spun peg-top (Figure 17). If Kaudern's specimens of sling-stones are typical, it was a remarkable observation by these islanders that a missile of that shape when given a rotary motion might be more accurately delivered than the conventional missile approximating a sphere. The difficulty is that Kaudern's sling-stones are unconventional; they are not worldwide in pattern. Kaudern felt that the origin of the top in these island cultures was not to be ascribed to outside cultures; tops were observed among tribes of the remote interior of large islands where these tribes had little or no contact with tribes nearer the coast.

The present writer, looking at the rich variety of top shapes

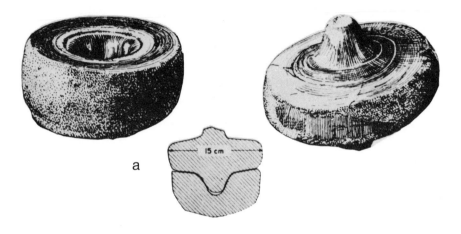

a

Figure 16. Likenesses of the top. (a) potter's wheel bearing from Jericho (based on Childe); (b) Malayan top (University of Pennsylvania Museum number 16189).

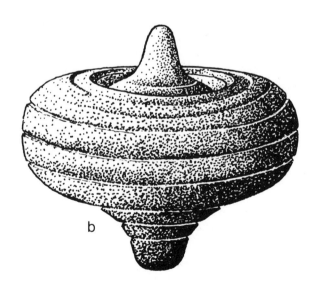

b

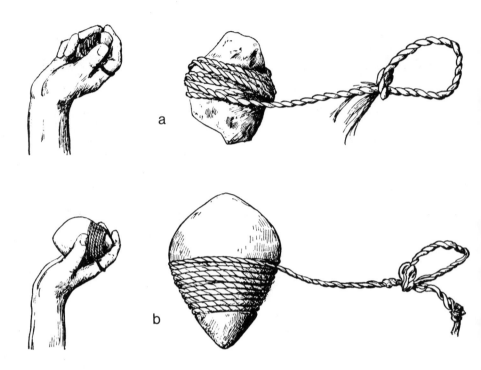

Figure 17. Sling-stone (a) and Celebes peg-top (b) from region of Lake Poso, Sulawesi (based on Kaudern).

throughout primitive cultures, feels that the top has originated spontaneously and independently many times over. If the specimens were put side by side, one might doubt whether some of them were good, that is, well-performing tops. But because we did not make these "poorer" tops and did not spin them to the exclusion of other types, there may be an injustice in downgrading them. The original maker might be a very deft operator.

In conclusion, it is unlikely that evidence will be found of the conventional top's invention or origin in prehistoric times.

Truly primitive cultures are shrinking rapidly and one can only hope that some prehistoric toys will survive and that they will be recognized as examples of early man's fascination with motion. History itself affords no clue as to the time and place of the top's invention. Early civilizations in Mesopotamia and Egypt, for example, possessed the toy, but although primitive races in the nineteenth and twentieth centuries have been found to have tops, there is little probability that knowledge of them was gained from the others. The Pacific Islands and all the continents except Antarctica have had tops, and it can hardly be argued that a trivial pastime spread from a common source, while other inventions vital to man's survival and progress were not similarly dispersed. It is our opinion that *play* brought the top into existence, and play assumes some respite from obvious dangers and the pressing needs of daily wants. Curiously, within historic times, some types of the top have been re-introduced in some areas as a novelty, presumably having disappeared for centuries. Some persons have credited the Japanese or Chinese with the top's invention, and attribute the renewal of European top-spinning to Dutch seaborne commerce with the Orient. Yet lore, art, and literature agree in antedating the top to such diffusion by Holland's mariners. The presence of the top in classical times has been described in another section.

BIBLIOGRAPHICAL REFERENCES

21, 63, 84, 109, 202, 221, 277, 307, 309, 344, 349

CHAPTER TWO

COMPLEXITIES

CITED BELOW are some of the aspects involved in spinning a top. The listing may not be complete; certainly the items could be regrouped many ways with equal logic.

These factors must include body effort of the spinner, whether the fingers, the palm, or the whole hand. The action may require a variety of efforts such as twisting, pulling, throwing, or tossing. It will be shown that outside forces such as light, magnetism, and explosions may impart motion to the top. Certain types of tops need to be supported when they are being started; some require support after being placed in motion.

With some tops, the required impulse to spin the top is imparted by a cord, or a whip, or a rod. Once the top is placed in motion, it may be allowed to spin until stopped by friction; or the motion may be sustained indefinitely by further effort of the spinner applied continuously or intermittently. Some types of tops permit bidirectional spinning.

In addition to these factors, there may be conditions where

special effects—optical, audio, or inertial—are sought. The use of the top for random decision-making and for divination is sometimes involved.

Out of this bewildering multitude of variables can be selected six patterns which seem to be deeply embedded in cultures, past and present. In these patterns we see: twisting action on a stem (or prolongation of the principal axis) is imparted by the hand(s) or fingers or, alternatively, by a cord; twisting action of a cord is imposed on the body of the top by casting the top or by whipping the top; bidirectional motion can be imparted to the top by twisting of cord or by the inertia of the top itself.

Examples of these six patterns are afforded in Figure 18:

a. *The Twirler* started by twisting action of fingers or hands upon the axis.

b. *The Supported-top* started by cord while top is held upright.

c. *The Peg-top* cast, and the twisting action of a cord on the body of the top imparts spin.

d. *The Whip-top* the body of the top is lashed to give continued motion.

e. *The Buzzer* * bidirectional motion through twisting of the cord.

f. *The Yo-yo* † bidirectional motion due to inertia and successive energy input.

* Many regard this as a noisemaker rather than as a top; the unconventional geometry notwithstanding, it has kinship with the yo-yo.

† Advertising not implied; see also Chapter 3.

►

Figure 18 (a-f). The six principal types of tops.

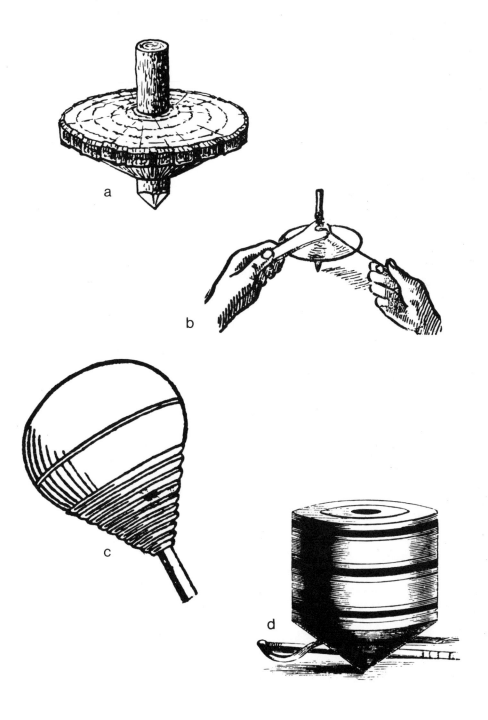

a

b

c

d

e

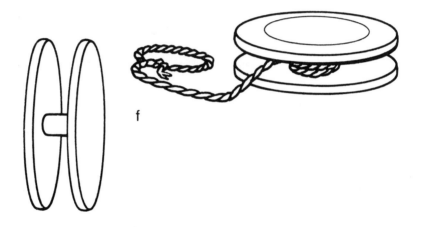

f

There is no intent to ascribe precedence in invention of these classes, nor can it be said that the presence of common elements denotes development of one form from another. A variant form could be invented independently in cultures that had no transmitted knowledge of it from other cultures.

Man's ingenuity has taken the elements of these six types and has made many combinations. Over seven hundred United

States patents * have been issued on tops as toys; many others have been credited to the gyroscope. If the result of these combinations sometimes subordinates the idea of the top as a toy, this is regrettable; the top has persisted because its principal use is as a toy.

In other sections specific tops and their effects will be discussed and reference will be made to the six principal types. But the reader must be constantly on the alert to recognize combinations and variations of the six types. (See Chapter 5 on plastics.)

A host of objections will arise, but in the interests of leading rather than propelling the reader into the complexities, the following attributes of a top are stressed: It moves around a principal axis, and the motion of rotation is large compared to the motion of translation; it is a toy in the sense that it is an amusement device and not an object associated with man's sterner needs.

Readers about seventy-five years ago were delighted by an article in *Scientific American*† signed "J.J." The article assumed the readers' familiarity with the subject. What may have been true then needs amplification now. (I am not sure about the author's identity but I think it may have been J. Jordan, a Frenchman whose primary interest was astronomy and whose ability to write lucidly on scientific subjects for the general reading public is impressive.) In the table I have put together, these tops are identified. The names assigned by me are consistent with those in the text to follow where many of the tops will be described in detail within the class or classes to which they belong. (See Figure 19.)

We have not used all the tops described by Jordan, but we have spun those believed to be analogous specimens patented and marketed within the past century.

* See Appendix 3.

† And in its French counterpart *La Nature*.

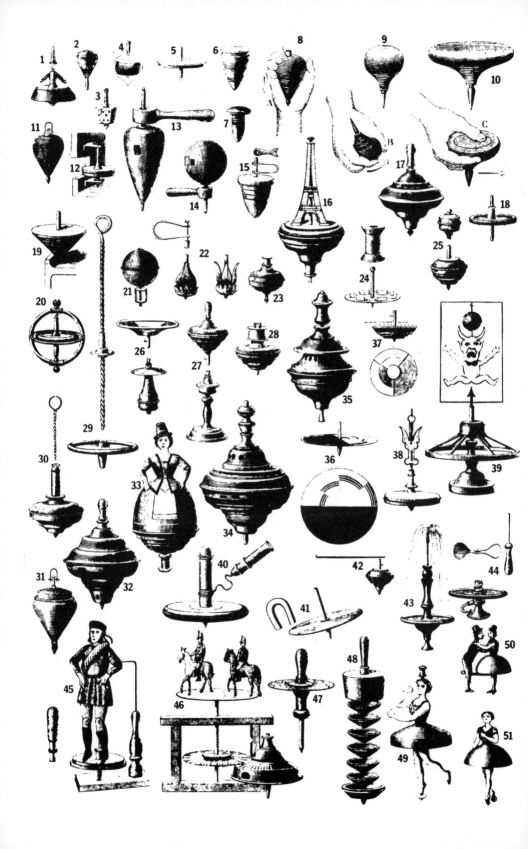

J.J. NUMBER	CLASS	J.J. NUMBER	CLASS
1	Twirler	24	Air-blown
2	Twirler (peg)	25	Twirler (spring)
3	Twirler (teetotum)	26	Aerial (spring)
4	Twirler	27	Spring
5	Twirler	28	Spring
6	Whipping	29	Aerial (helix)
7	Whipping	30	Helix
8	Holding position	31	Swivel (peg)
9	Peg (holding position)	32	Helix (humming)
		33	Helix
10	Peg	34	Helix (musical)
11	Peg (swivel)	35	Helix (musical)
12	Supported-in-starting	36	Color disc
		37	Color disc
13	Supported-in-starting	38	Expanding
		39	Expanding
14	Supported-in-starting	40	Novelty
		41	Magnetic
15	Supported-in-starting	42	Magnetic
		43	Supported
16	Helix (supported)	44	Helix (aerial)
17	Helix	45	Supported
18	Twirler (supported)	46	Supported
19	Supported	47	Barus gyrograph
20	Gyroscope	48	Multiple
21	Restrained yo-yo	49	Supported
22	Supported	50	Supported
23	Supported	51	Supported

Figure 19. Display of nineteenth-century tops (based on J.J.).

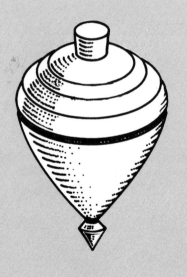

CHAPTER THREE

SIX PRINCIPAL TYPES CLASSIFIED

SIX IMPORTANT types of tops and six patterns of imparting and maintaining motion in tops have evolved. The same number of patterns and of types is accidental; there is no direct relationship of one group with the other. Here, the characteristics of the principal types of tops and their interplay with one or more means of imparting motion will be developed. Some variants of tops are included, but usually are subordinated. The Patent Office records are adequate evidence of crossbreeding of the basic characteristics. (See Appendix 3.)

DESCRIPTION OF THE SIX PRINCIPAL TYPES OF TOPS AND MANNER OF SPINNING THEM

TYPE 1 THE TWIRLER

The twirler is a top spun by twisting action on the stem by hands or fingers. Common variants are an impaled berry or nut and the teetotum (Figure 20). All the tops in the figure are readily put in motion by twisting the stem with thumb and fingers of one hand. The stem is most commonly above the body of the top as, for example, in (a) and (b), where the axis is prolonged to the other side to provide a bearing point. Or the stem may be below the body as in (f) and itself provides the bearing point. The teetotum (j) is discussed in a later section where its function as a "decision-maker" will be unfolded.

A top comparable to Figure 20, item (g), may be spun to give rotation for perhaps twenty to thirty seconds. But the reader can perform an interesting experiment to prolong this spinning indefinitely! Spin the top (with clockwise rotation) on a wooden plate; as the top slows, give the plate a rotary, counterclockwise motion, moving the plate so that its center describes a circle about the peg of the top. The experimenter will discover the adverse effects of clockwise rotation of the plate or the use of a smooth-surfaced plate. (See also precession discussed later under Technical Aspects of the Top.)

Figure 21 shows a scene dated to classical times. The person is watching something intently. The object has been called variously a buzzer, a magic wheel, a rhombus, and a twirler; the last term seems suitable. There appears to be a disc, and an

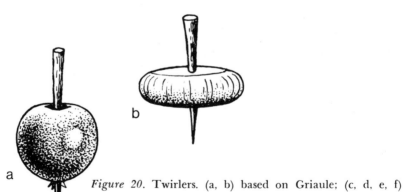

Figure 20. Twirlers. (a, b) based on Griaule; (c, d, e, f) based on Culin; (g, h, i, j) after J.J.

40

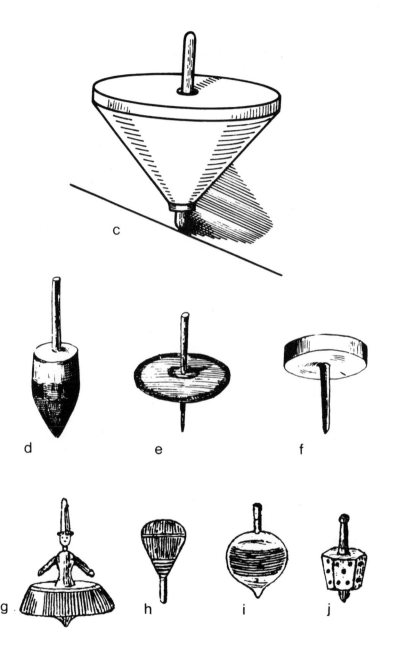

c

d   e   f

g   h   i   j

axle pointed at both ends. Were both ends used as bearing points? If so, this suggests that the upper surface or plane was in view as the top spun and was significantly marked. Possibly the top was used in divination or perhaps just to indulge in unabashed fascination with motion. Or, more mundane, as a gambling device? The teetotum is a child of the top, and is a variant of the twirler. Finally, with no evidence to sustain the idea, one might use the shafted top of Figure 21 with the kind of support shown in Figure 26. No such holding device has been found in classical art or archaeology and there is no proof as to whether the invention of the top preceded that of the wheel, but one may say that the top has appeared in many cultures where the wheel was unknown.

The most primitive twirlers and perhaps the first tops capable of rapid rotation may have been a seed or fruit impaled by a thorn. Such twirlers made in childhood are, without doubt, ancient in origin and amazingly persistent in all cultures. The wooden toy from India (Figure 18a) can be spun by a child to rotate for twenty seconds and cost perhaps a quarter of a cent.

Two important games of childhood were invented for this kind of top: to place a given number of such tops in motion together; and to set a top in motion and require that some objective be reached before the top's motion ceases.

Development of piercing and cutting tools enabled further use of larger, harder-shelled nuts, and longer, shaped stems. Probably the observation was made that a larger and heavier top performed better; the spinning was steadier and of longer duration. This was due, of course, to two things: greater momentum accompanying the greater weight had diminished the relative effect of friction at the bearing point in contact with the ground; and symmetry and balance were more readily achieved.

The extension and strengthening of the stem rising above the body of the top enabled the player to roll the stem between the palms of the hands. This created a top that has had wide favor (Figure 14). The suggestion has been made that the palm motion was derived from a fire-making device.

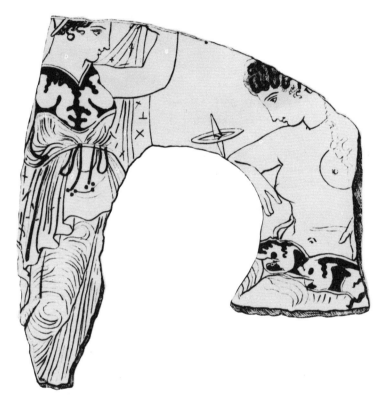

Figure 21. Fragment of ceramic decoration showing twirler;
classical scene (based on Jahn).

THE TEETOTUM

As classified in this study, the teetotum is a twirler, that is, a top spun by twisting the axis with the fingers. The body may be a disc, a polygonal plate, or a polyhedron (Figure 22). Since classical times, the device has been an adjunct to games of chance and is most commonly associated with such play, however innocent of gain-motive. Early and perhaps original forms of the teetotum were cubes whose four vertical faces were inscribed respectively: T (for *totum*) all, that is, take everything staked; A (for *aufer*) take (by custom) half the stakes; D (for *depone*) put (an additional amount into the pool); N (for *nihil*) that is the player neither puts nor takes.

The inscription on the faces of the body may change with the nationality adopting the toy. In France, this top has been known as *le toton* (Figure 23).* Simpler forms might be marked with the letters: T, *tout*; A, *accipe* or P, *prend*; D, *donne*; R, *rien*; while in Germany the top may be called *Trendel* (from *trenden* to turn) and the lettering appears as: G, *ganz*; H, *halb*; S, *stellen*; N, *nichts*. The Jewish *dreidel*, or *dredl*, may carry Hebrew or roman script letters. (See also account of use in Hanukkah celebration in this section.)

* *Je qui tourne soubz autruy main*
  Nay seurete ne soir ne main
  Car al soubz quelle main ie tourne
  Si soudainement sen retourne
  Quil natent ne hui ne demain.

I who spin under another man's hand
Have no security morning nor evening
For under whosoever's hand I spin
He turns away so suddenly he waits
  neither for today or tomorrow.
        (Courtesy M. Gutwirth, Haverford College)

►

Figure 22. Teetotums. (a) Oriental; (b) German; (c) Korean, with notches used instead of characters (University of Pennsylvania Museum number 17627); (d) Hanukkah-type *dreidel*.

a

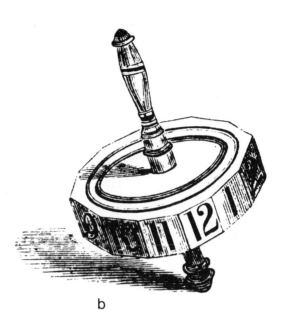

b

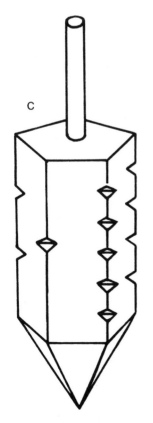

c

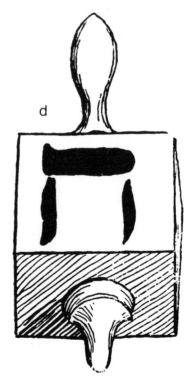

d

LA PIROVETE

Ie quj tourne soubz autruy main
Nay seurete ne soir ne main
Car al soubz quelle main ie tourne
Et soudainement sen retourne
Quil natent ne huy ne demain

LE JEU DU TOTON OU DE LA PIROUETTE

The sequence of the significant signs on the faces has usually been that of "take all," "take half," "put," "no action," although there are minor unexplained exceptions. The reader will recall that the number of pips on opposite sides of a die cube will always total seven. The body of a top has been known with more than four faces; this is an obvious extension to the use of a die with six faces. The custom seems to have prevailed that the uppermost character appearing when the top fell to rest should govern the play.

Gomme [152] discussing the game of teetotum in Scotland, indicates that it was played by children of either sex, and only at Christmastime; the stakes were pins. A parallel Hanukkah pastime has been ascribed to copying the Christian custom; the ascription is questionable. A visitor to London in 1864 writes with delight to a friend in Hungary that he has just seen a toy called a "Teetotum." He says it was exactly like a Hanukkah *dreidel (Trendel)* with English letters instead of Hebrew. "But why it is called by its peculiar name (Tee-to-tum) no one can tell us." He was, of course, looking at the toy, a lineal descendant from classical times. The Hanukkah-permitted top was often inscribed with Hebrew characters. It was a favorite with the Jews of Germany and Poland. The letters S, N, G, H would reflect the dual background of the players. These letters have names which convey the same meaning as the common teetotum: G (*ganz* or *gimel*), the player takes all the pool; H (*halb* or *heh*), the player takes half the pool; S (*stell* or *schin*), the worst, that is, the player adds to the pool; N (*nichts* or *nun*), nothing is added to or taken from the pool.

Various accounts that purport to read a more mystic significance into the symbols are generally discounted by Jewish

◄

Figure 23. Le toton.

scholars. The top was not looked upon as a means of serious gambling; to profit from its play was not honorable. Yet its use among children was without great objection by the rabbis and elders, and was accounted part of the festival season. In this season, the exchange of gifts may be common, and children may be given Hanukkah *gelt*, i.e., small money. The origin, then, of the Hanukkah top is uncertain. It has been postulated that the use of the teetotum was an observed practice among Christians at their major holiday season, and so adopted by the Hebrews. This does not seem tenable, or at least not wholly acceptable. There was plenty of opportunity for the diffusion of the Hanukkah practice from mid-Europe to the British Isles. It is probable that the gambling die in the form of the teetotum followed the Roman legions, and the diffusion throughout Europe might be expected to be accomplished in a few centuries. In the Hanukkah festival we may confidently look upon the top in its foremost role—a toy and a pastime for children. Solis-Cohen and Gerson [315] give a puppet-play, *The Magic Top*, using the four-faced Hanukkah top as one of the principals. The substance and mood of the play reflect a festive occasion for children. And we have seen Hanukkah objects whose size and balance precluded their use as tops; their function was to serve as a container (as for candy).

The teetotum provides an apt phrase recurring in English literature; comment upon the equating of the top to human behavior is given elsewhere. The reader should ponder the mystery of a toy whose significance in coming to rest is infinitely greater than when in full motion. Of all the variants of the top, the teetotum seems to have had the maximum of interest in use; it possesses simplicity of design and operation; it seems to have a future without a foreseeable end.

THE TIPPE TOP

This top, shown in Figure 24 and carrying the imprint "British Pat. Appl. 656540," has been marketed in recent years and has

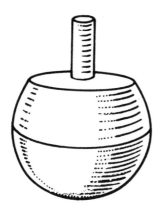

Figure 24. The Tippe Top (British Patent Application 656540).

generated an unusual amount of technical interest. We were afforded an opportunity to try the top, courtesy of Dr. J. A. Jacobs.[208] The specimen weighed 9.6 grams (less than one-half ounce). Placed casually upon a horizontal surface, it assumes the attitude of the above figure, indicating a low center of gravity. If the knurled stem is grasped between the thumb and forefinger, with the stem in a downward position, the top is readily spun. So readily does it spin that a child can quickly attain proficiency. It seems that this must be the secret of the top, and that the acclaim given it is the voiced satisfaction of many persons who never became adept with conventional tops.

But the most fascinating feature, and the source of its name, is the ability to invert itself when spun vigorously on its rounded body (stem up). This attention-getting toy is an excellent extension of the psychological satisfaction that follows when an object assumes an un-natural (un-understood) position. When this top passes from rotation on its rounded body to rotation on its stem, it actually passes to the position of, say, a peg-top spinning vigorously. The geometry of the peg-top precludes a rise onto the peg if the top is started with the body in contact with the ground; the smooth, rounded surface of the Tippe Top enables the reversal.

This top has had adequate mathematical attention. Copley [81] felt that the Tippe Top was no novelty and that a similar object described forty years earlier was the equivalent. Then, Perry [272] had presented a wholly spherical object that, when spun vigorously, always assumed a position with a distinctive marking uppermost. Presumably the sphere was so weighted on the bias (as by a plug) that the center of gravity was not the geometrical center. My Tippe Top has a hollow stem and a cavity in the body (Figure 35, item a). The effect of overall dimensions on the performance of the top has not been reported. Gordon [154] describes the enthusiasm with which the top was received in the Scandinavian countries: "persons great and notable relished its play."

TYPE 2   THE TOP SET IN MOTION BY A CORD WHILE THE TOP IS SUPPORTED

The progression from the simplest twirler (Figure 18 a) to the long-stemmed top (Figure 14) where a brisk sliding motion between the hands is used was no small achievement. Perhaps the fire-drill bow led to the next advance, that of turning the stem of the top with a bowstring. At any rate this technique was tried and it proved successful. Note that in this case the stem is supported or constrained so that very little lateral movement is possible. The bowstring gives a bidirectional rotation if the string is kept taut; if the cord is relaxed on alternate strokes, unidirectional motion results. In neither case is very high speed of rotation attained.

A further, highly important development occurred when a cord was wound snugly for several turns about a supported top stem and the free end pulled smartly, setting the top into rapid rotation. A variant of this, which does not use a mechanical support, was also created. It required a *doubled* cord wound about the stem (Figure 25). When the two ends of the string are pulled in opposite directions by lateral movement of the hands, the top is spun and the cord comes free of the stem. This method has been reported prevalent in certain regions to the virtual exclusion of other methods. There are some difficulties with the method only overcome by practice and dexterity: The cord when wound in double fashion about the stem has a

Figure 25. Double-wound cord on long-stemmed top usually needing a support or bracket (University of Pennsylvania Museum number 22753).

tendency to loosen as the top is being set in an upright position (the novice will wish for a third hand to support the top and will probably call for an assistant); and because it is difficult to impart equal pull on the ends of the cord, the spindle's footing is often displaced laterally from the intended point of contact with the ground. However, the above drawbacks can be overcome in part, and this top spins faster and longer than the simple twirler.

DEVELOPMENT OF SPECIALIZED SUPPORT

At some point there was a tremendous improvement. It was a tool to be held by the operator which would perform one or more functions simultaneously: it would support the top in a vertical position until the top acquired sufficient speed to stand upright itself, prevent lateral displacement while the cord was being pulled, and offer a counterbalance to the human effort in pulling the cord. The instrument was an achievement of the first order, and it has been re-invented (and patented) over and over again (Figure 26). The device has been called by many names: a key, bracket, yoke, sprocket, lift-off-tool, grip, holder, cage, handle, and so on. Some tops are spun so that the stem of the spinning top remains within the confines of the device, but in most cases the device will be lifted from the stem as soon as the cord is withdrawn. Thus was born the "humming-top"; the speed of rotation was sufficiently high that holes or irregularities in the top's surface produced a pleasant hum. The supported-in-starting top has proved to be one of the most popular toys. It can be spun successfully by any person after a couple of demonstrations, which is not true of such tops as the whip-top, peg-top, and yo-yo.

The brackets shown in Figures 26, 27, and 28 represent a very special tool. It has been noted that some cultures used a bit of wood or shell with a hole in it through which the cord was withdrawn while the left hand held the object against the

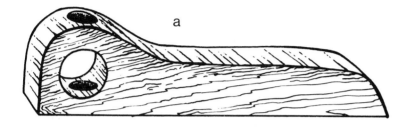

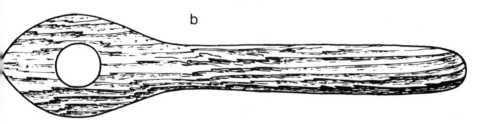

Figure 26. Brackets or supports. (a) modern; (b) nineteenth-century (University of Pennsylvania Museum number 21315).

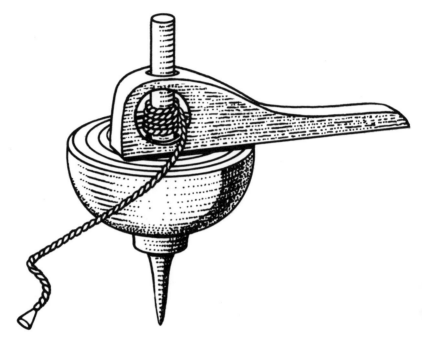

Figure 27. Supported-top and bracket, showing cord in place (University of Pennsylvania Museum number 22753).

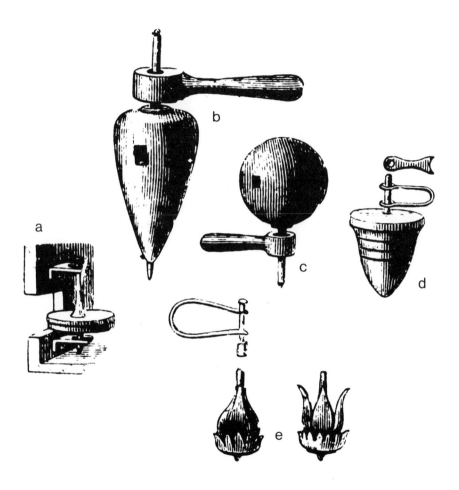

Figure 28. Supported-tops (after J.J.).

top which was in a vertical position. This innovation seemingly followed the practice of using the fingers themselves in contact with the stem to offer resistance to the lateral displacement of the top when the cord was withdrawn. We have pondered (and practiced a bit) as to whether the stemmed, supported top could be given continuous motion as is possible with the whip-top (see Type 4). Without gaining great proficiency, we concluded that it was feasible and might be performed in the following way: The top is started in the usual manner, but the bracket is not withdrawn. Of course friction at the stem and air resistance upon the body of the top will cause a progressive deceleration. Now suppose that a simple turn or two of the cord is taken about the stem, caution being used that the winding is in the same rotational direction as the revolving top; the bracket is anchored in place or is held by a second person. The operator uses his left hand to hold the free end of the cord to offer some slight resistance against the withdrawal of the cord by the right hand and thereby bring the cord snugly about the stem. Here is an opportunity to develop teamwork such as is possible with the whip-top. Having made this discovery, we then found that a Japanese toy gyroscope carried much the same instructions, the frame of the gyroscope, of course, being the equivalent of a bracket. A single turn of the cord about the gyroscope axle is made while the hand holding the frame also restrains moderately the pull exerted upon the cord by the other hand.

Examples of tops which are supported in starting are shown in Figure 28, derived from J. J.'s assembly (Figure 19). Items (b) and (c) are familiar. With item (c), it is best to wind the cord with successive turns upward between the point and the support. As the cord is withdrawn, the top rises in the support and jumps free to spin on the table. Item (d) is notable for the simplicity of the lift-off support. Item (a) is a supported-in-starting top where the support is quite rigid and a tremendous pull can be exerted on the string in starting. Stronger supports allow the cord to be drawn horizontally away from the top. The two supports are slotted so that after the cord is withdrawn, the top may be pushed away from the supports to rotate freely. Item (e) is sometimes called "Flora." The body has an elongated upper stem which is threaded loosely into the lower end of the shaft of the support. The shaft itself can rotate freely in the yoke. The yoke and support do not lift off when the top is placed in motion, but when the yoke is squeezed to put restraint on the shaft, it causes the top, because of inertia, to unscrew from the shaft's end and drop free. The ornaments, such as leaves or petals, are spread outward by centrifugal force (Figure 28 e).

James Clerk Maxwell's interest * in tops included his experiments in light and, particularly, human vision. In a paper [254] he described the ability of the human eye to distinguish mixed colors. Figure 29 depicts his apparatus. Discs, each of a single color, were mounted on a spindle and became the equivalent of the body of a top. When the assembly was spun, the colors seemed to merge, and produced effects which were repeatable. It will be noted that the discs in Figure 29 (a,b) can be overlapped to give any chosen proportion of exposure. The response of the eye to changing proportions greatly aided in an understanding of color-blindness.

DEVELOPMENT OF REVERSING MOTION

In the preceding discussion of the supported top, it was assumed that the string was wound about the stem of the top but not tied to the stem. A remarkable variant of play may be obtained by modifying the usual operation. Tie the free end of

* Maxwell was primarily a physicist, often concerned with energy and its propagation. The novel development of his theories rested on voluminous and (to us) abstruse mathematics. His solution of problems received and deserved the term "elegant." He, too, became interested in the analogy of the gyroscope to the Earth, and he designed a complex instrument for this study and wrote a paper "on a dynamical top, for exhibiting the phenomenon of the motion of invariable form about a fixed point, with some suggestions as to the Earth's motion." Maxwell never spared a word or an algebraic equation to make his subject lucid.

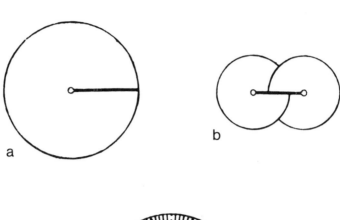

a

b

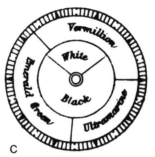

c

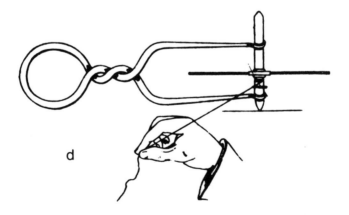

d

the cord to the axis of the top and wind the cord about the stem. While using one hand to hold the support, use the other hand to pull on the string thereby unwinding the cord from the stem. Just before complete unwinding takes place, relax the pull on the cord. The top will have been set spinning and its inertia will cause it to continue spinning and to rewind the cord in the opposite direction. A second pull on the cord will cause the top to rotate as for the first pull. The result is captivating. We might call the top's action recuperative because inertia has caused the top to rewind itself. The total action is that of a vigorous pull to unwind the cord and spin the top, followed by a "coasting" of the top to rewind the cord.

This type of top and the buzzer (Type 5) can be manipulated by the player to make frequent reversals, an impossibility with the twirler, the peg-top, and the whip-top. Figure 30 shows how this principle works: a few sprigs of flowers are bound to the shaft; when set in rapid rotation the effect is a mass of color. Because there is an alternate pull-relaxation sequence, the pull

◄

Figure 29 (a-d). One of Maxwell's simpler color tops. The proportions of the several discs exposed are readily adjusted. The resulting merged color seen by the eye is a function of the degree of color-blindness.

Figure 30. Recuperative yo-yo. (a) based on J.J.; (b) cross-section of a nut perforated to receive shaft and cord (based on Béart).

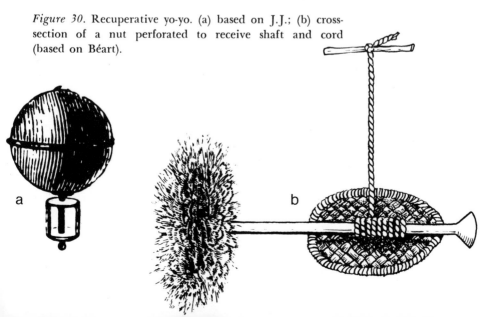

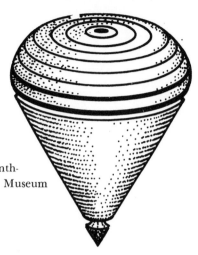

Figure 31. Peg-top; German, nineteenth-century (University of Pennsylvania Museum number 18277).

upon the cord must be relatively gentle. As high speed cannot be obtained as with the free cord, audio effects will be less. But this type of top lends itself to rhythm because of the successive reversals. It is a toy well suited to the sedentary and non-adventurous because it is always within the grasp of the owner. Some writers have termed this type of top a "yo-yo" because it exhibits the reversible motion of the well known toy. In distinguishing this top from the yo-yo we point out that the cord takes on translation while the top passively remains in place but takes on rotation, whereas the true yo-yo takes on both translation and rotation.

TYPE 3   THE PEG-TOP

With some exceptions, the peg-top has a pear-shaped body (Figure 31). The name itself is ambiguous since the peg is optional rather than essential. In this study, the peg-top will refer to the top on which a cord is wound that is then cast or thrown free of the cord, thereby setting the top in rapid rotation on the ground. It is the queen of tops and not to be slighted. It lends itself to competition in the sense that the player's skill can be measured. The toy was known to many primitive cultures and has had much usage among European peoples. Because of its simplicity, Henry Allemagne [3] felt that the peg-top was derived from the whip-top (Type 4) and he cites a writer who says that the peg-top was invented to provide a toy requiring less strenuous exertion than the whip-top (a coddling which the writer disapproved).

THE TOP PROPER

Shown in Figure 33 are several nineteenth-century peg-tops. Some of them resemble whip-tops (Figure 45) and, in fact, may have been intended or used as such. Contrasted to the whip-top that has retained its cone shape through thousands of years, the peg-top exhibits a fine variety of sizes and shapes. Figure 32, item (b), has a profile so flat that, to allow the cord to come free of the body, the top is cast with more horizontal motion than ordinarily. Tops like this have been made with cylindrical rather than tapering pegs and have performed well as supported tops (Type 2). They can range from discus-like form to a bulbous affair almost as broad as it is high. If the height and diameter are less than two inches (5 cm) the spinner will probably have

Figure 32. Peg-tops (based on J.J.). Bodies are wooden; pegs are steel.

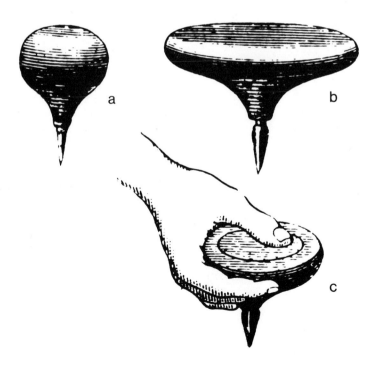

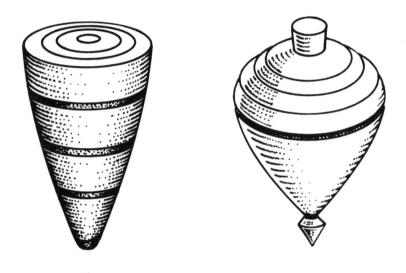

Figure 33. Peg-tops, nineteenth century; some may be used as whip-tops (specimens from University of Pennsylvania Museum).

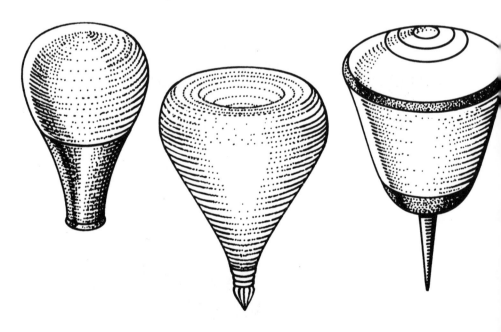

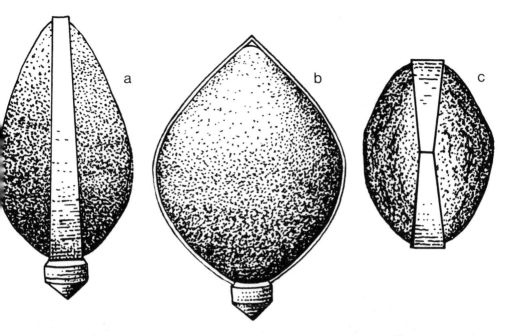

Figure 34. Three views of a peg-top of non-circular cross-section from Mindanao, Philippines. (a) side; (b) front; (c) view from above (University of Pennsylvania Museum number P3020).

trouble making the top perform properly; if the top is too large, it will require too much strength to cast it.

As with all tops, symmetry and balance are aids to duration of spinning. Because the top is subject to shock of impact when cast, a hard, clear wood is the usual construction material. The body is sometimes scored to assist holding the cord. For an interesting account of the manufacture of common peg-tops, see Fisher.[123] Figure 34 shows an anomaly in tops. The top (hand-carved) is symmetrical, but the cross-section about its principal axis is intentionally non-circular. Because of its shape, the top has a tendency to move away from its initial point of impact, a desirable feature in some games. The top is an early twentieth-century Filipino toy and one of a group, that is, it is not unique. An iron peg seems optional. It is likely that sound or sight effects also were sought in spinning these tops. The deterioration of the specimens precluded critical testing.

THE PEG

The peg is not functional to actual spinning of the peg-top, and, indeed, in early specimens, the spinning contact point was integral with the body, merely the sharpened end of the body. Later, insets of hardwood or bone were used, and finally a metallic tip. A brad, pin, or nail would serve (Figures 35 and 36). It could be driven into the body, threaded (very secure), or the shank might be cemented in an axial hole drilled in the body. Because the peg presents a small, smooth surface at the

Figure 35. X-ray display of metal pegs in peg-tops. (a) is wholly of plastic (Hospital, University of Pennsylvania).

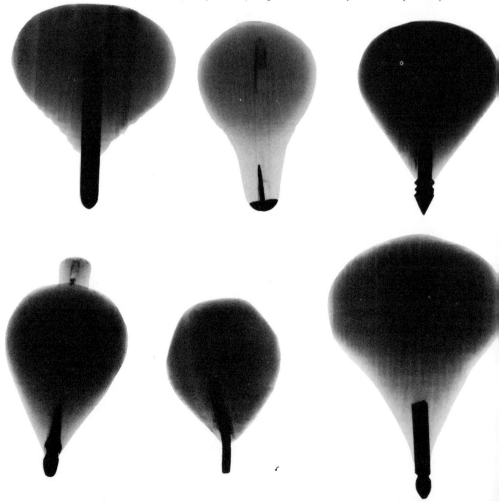

point of contact with the ground, loss of speed due to friction is much reduced. The peg has had secondary use as a means of inflicting injury on other tops; herewith a reminiscence of my own on the matter:

Springtime madness occasionally beset the boys, top-spinning descended to top-fighting. The intent was to hurt the opponents' tops; your own was cast with every hope of inflicting lasting scars. Seldom, however, was any opponent's top injured; vigor of casting overcame accuracy of aim. If the target area was

anything but dirt, the thrown top sustained a tremendous impact upon its peg. To lose a peg in action was a doubly sore grief: the top was rendered useless to its owner, and superiority of the opponent was tacitly admitted. It became a canon of faith that a top whose peg was set, that is, cemented in place by fresh horse manure was incapable of losing its peg. A newly-purchased top therefore must have its peg removed and then repacked with droppings from the nearest street. It made no difference that some of the pegs were threaded and incapable of suddenly losing their hold upon the top's body; at tremendous effort, the peg must be drawn and reset, thereby acquiring permanence of union. Any subsequent loss of peg in combat did not detract from the virtue of the formula; the weakness was scornfully ascribed to ineptness in re-setting the peg.*

As for injuries sustained in these contests, only two major incidents were ever noted by this observer: once when a top spinning in the ring was struck squarely on its upper surface and a large chip was broken out; the second, where a formidable "split-peg top" was sundered by the peg itself when the top was cast and the peg hit squarely upon a pebble.

Throughout the popular literature of the top runs a persistent trend to pit the top against its kind to inflict injury. Further comment and opinion will be found in Chapter 7, in the section "The Top as Weapon."

THE CORD

Here we must speak in generalities. A top two inches in diameter and two inches high may be spun with a five-foot length of No. 15 cord (approximately 1.7 mm); a top six inches in diameter would need ten feet or more of No. 120 cord (ap-

---

* The curious faith or dependence on coarse rites has an echo in some observations of boys' contests by Esquieu.[115] He says that the order of play in certain contests was determined as follows: one boy would spit on the ground and whoever cast his top to strike the spittle was given prime position. He also relates that boys would sometimes place their tops in the path of a heavily loaded wagon so that a wheel would pass over the tops. Any top that survived this punishment was envied; its virtue was self-evident.

proximately 4 mm). Some spinners of large, heavy tops will splice pieces of different diameter, using the lighter cord for the first turns on the top. The end first applied to the top is knotted to stop unraveling; the end held by the spinner is provided with a button. In examining museum specimens from more primitive cultures, it has been our impression that coarse cords, heavier than necessary, were used. Whether this was consistent with available vegetable fibers or whether it was a proved practice yielding very effective top-spinning, we cannot say. Most of the cords, now upwards of seventy-five years old, have lost their strength. The tops respond well to our present-day cordages, including synthetics. The table below shows some cordage sizes:

	DIAMETER	
SIZE NUMBER	*Inches*	*Centimeters*
9	.032	.081
21	.060	.152
60	.103	.261
108	.140	.355
330	.250	.632

SPINNING THE TOP

So many tops are described in this book that the reader might well suppose the author to have some skill in spinning. Sadly, this is not so, and although the author has spun virtually every type of top, adeptness has not followed. This was evident when he tried a group of tops of similar shape but of different dimension and weight. The single-purposiveness of a child at play is needed, and the frequently made observation by nineteenth-century authors that ". . . this top is valued above all others; nothing can induce him to trade or sell it" is appreciated, and doubtless is an attitude of mind that follows one's mastery of the requirements of a particular top.

To describe how to spin a top is a task to inhibit the bravest man. Ask any young top-spinner how to spin a peg-top and his reply, after a puzzled moment, is "like this." You can't really tell someone how to do it. In this book, the would-be spinner is brought within sight of the objective, handed a list of instructions, and told to go ahead. The instructor then disappears, wondering whether the written word gathered from several sources is really helpful; he never used it, for he acquired the knowledge without realizing how it was imparted.

Two methods seem to have found favor in Europe and later in America. These differ in three basic ways: of imposing and winding the cord, in how the top is held, and in casting the top. Inevitably methods overlap and lend themselves to variations. These will undoubtedly be discovered by the zealous top-spinner.

GENERAL INSTRUCTIONS

Choose a cleared spot of hard-packed soil or, better, a floor area several feet square. Provide a "backstop" or a wall protected by a cloth. We will presume the top-spinner to be right-handed. Hold the top with the left hand, with the peg pointing to the right. The knotted end of the cord should be placed against the side of the top about half the distance from the peg to the normal upper surface of the top and held there by the left thumb. Take the line to the base of the peg and start winding the cord about the top in a counter-current direction (the cord will come toward you from the under side). There is usually a depression between the shank of the peg and the top's body which will receive and anchor the first turn of the string. Draw each turn taut—how taut, trial alone must determine. Successive turns, spiraling upward around the top, should not overlap. From ten to twenty turns may be taken, and the free (knotted) end of the cord should be firmly bound to the top by the coils. Hold the button end of the string between the middle and third fingers of the right hand, the button resting on the outside of the fingers. If there is much excess cord, take one or more turns about the hand. The top is now shifted to the grasp of the right hand. Winding the cord in the manner prescribed enables a spinner to keep the cord tighter during this shift.

METHOD I

Hold the top around its body with the thumb and fingers. Squat, bringing the top, peg down, to about a foot above the floor (see Figure 36). Move the wrist and forearm smartly away from the body, at the same time giving them a rolling motion which flips the top causing it to make a complete turn in space. This snap motion is ended with a moderate whip-like pull on the string, setting the top in full rotation on its peg. This method is fairly reliable but does not lend itself to high rotational speed.

METHOD II

This second method of casting, once mastered, allows greater accuracy of placement and higher rotational speed. It has two variants. In one, the top is held in the left hand and the cord applied as before except that the winding may be in either

Figure 36. Setting the peg-top in motion, elementary method.

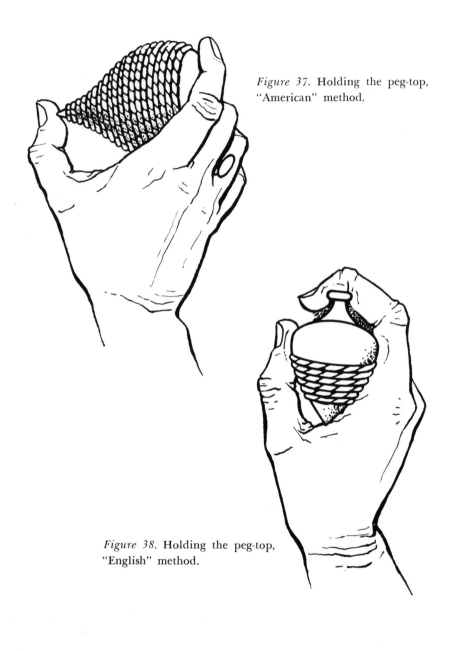

Figure 37. Holding the peg-top, "American" method.

Figure 38. Holding the peg-top, "English" method.

direction. After the cord is tautly wound, the top is held in the right hand with the thumb at the peg, and with the first two fingers upon the upper surface of the top's head (Figure 37). Or the top may be snuggled by the side of the thumb and the hand (Figure 38). The raised arm is swept down and forward, releasing the top at a point calculated to place the top in an upright position several feet in front of the spinner. The most skillful performers impart a nice proportion of throwing action and of whip-withdrawal of the cord at the correct moment when making this cast; this is an advanced technique. The person who masters the overhand cast will discover his own techniques.

The other variant requires that the top be held in the left hand and the free end of the cord placed at or near the normal upper surface of the top. The line is carried up and wound counterclockwise around the upper vertical portion of the top. Making a turn across the cord, the line is carried down to the peg and wound spirally in a counterclockwise direction. The cord is kept taut by the button as before and the top is shifted to the right hand. One must then hold the top, peg up, before him, raise the extended arm behind and somewhat above the head. Then with a sidearm motion, the top is thrown forward and down, and let loose at the point estimated to cause the pegpoint to strike the ground cleanly. This method is good in respect to accuracy of placement.

The peg-top has a curious variant (Figure 39). In effect, this variant has a swivel at its upper end with one end of the cord tied securely to the swivel. The cord is drawn down to and wound up from the peg's root in either direction. The top can then be dropped and if the correct vertical distance is allowed for, the top will spin at the player's feet. When the top dies, it will not roam far. Contemptuously, we boys used to call it a girl's top; this feeling was heightened because of our frustration at not being able to snatch the tops from their rightful owners. It was nettling, too, to see almost invariable success in spinning this top. Not for some time did we learn of and appreciate that

Figure 39. Variant of the peg-top, having a swivel at its upper end. The free end of a cord is tied upon the swivel and is then carried down to the peg for winding; button end of cord is held as usual.

this top could show a remarkable effect: the top if wound and spun as described above would create a path (Figure 41 b). If the cord is so held that the top does not touch the ground when dropped, the peg makes the still different path (Figure 41 c). If the top is thrown down, rather than dropped, it will spin with enough velocity so that the major axis is parallel to the ground. If the top is allowed to sink so that the peg touches the ground, the path's direction is reversed. To the technically minded, the paths illustrate precession. Mechanically inclined scientists have captured the tracings of these tops with such instruments as the gyrograph. (See Figure 19, item 47,* and Figure 42.)

It is justly pointed out that the peg-top should spin for a long time were it not for the effects of friction between the peg and the ground and also that friction caused by the drag of the air itself. On ice or glass, or in a chamber from which the air has been evacuated there is ample confirmation of this, and a duration of spinning for over one hour has been reported. Upon

---

* Obviously a supported-in-starting top. At least one made by Prof. Barus [19] about seventy years ago has survived and is in the collection of the late Dr. J. W. Wilson.

Figure 40. Twentieth-century peg-top with swivel (courtesy of the late J. W. Wilson).

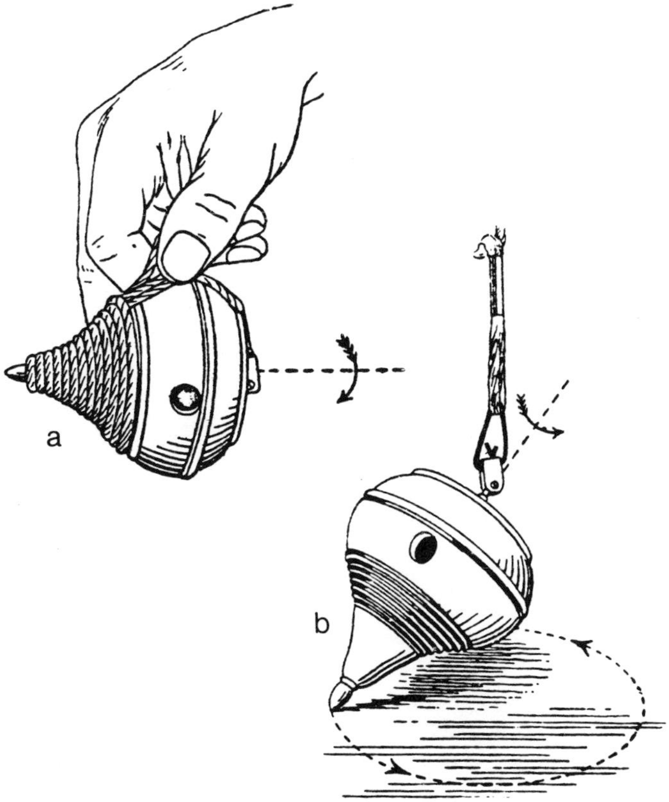

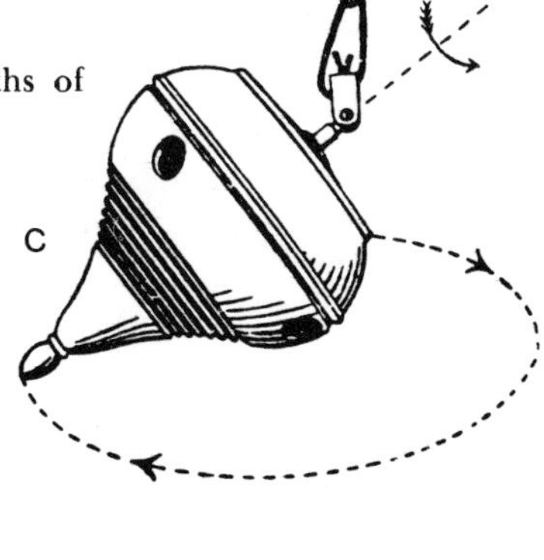

Figure 41. (a) proper winding of cord and (b,c) paths of top illustrating precession (after Crabtree).

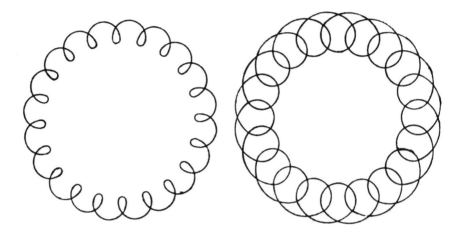

Figure 42. Representative curves traced by precessing top.

consideration, this would seem likely only with a massive, finely machined top, initially placed in motion at very high speed.

SEPARABLE TOPS

We have never had the top represented by (b) in Figure 43, but we have tried the Trip-L-top (U.S. Patent number 2619769). Made of plastic, and fairly well balanced, it separated into its three components with a pleasing clatter, each spinning smoothly. The directions for imposing the cord are shown in Figure 44; the top is held in a horizontal position at the upper end by the thumb (at peg) and the last three fingers. The top is cast with an overhand motion.

a

Figure 43 (a-c). Separable tops. (a) French top (based on Champlin and Bostwick).

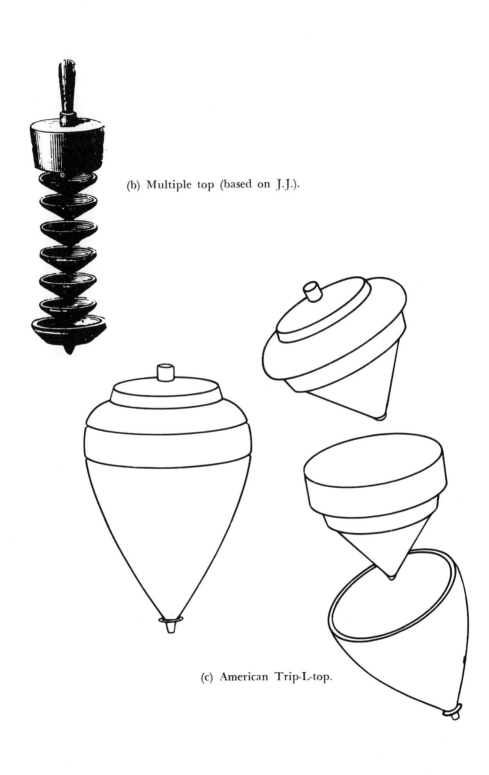

(b) Multiple top (based on J.J.).

(c) American Trip-L-top.

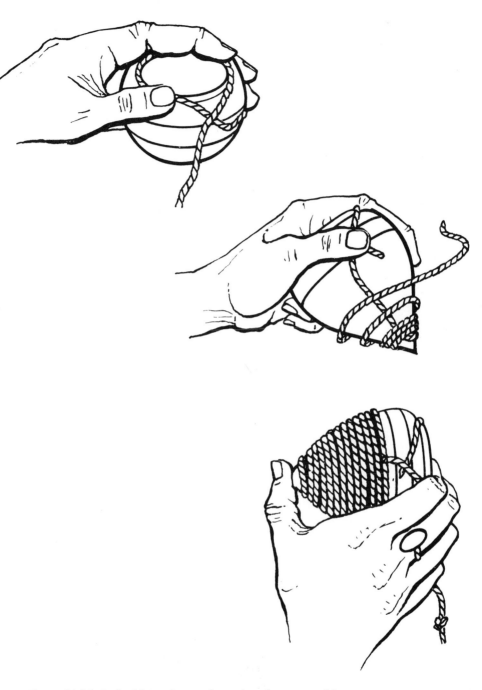

Figure 44. Method of imposing cord on American separable top.

TYPE 4   THE WHIP-TOP

The whip-top has retained, with few exceptions, its shape through millennia (Figure 45). Some of them so resemble the cone—the pine-cone—that the near likeness of their two names *strobos* and *strombos* seems a happy accident. There is nothing complicated about the design or construction; the bearing-point must withstand wear, but it is not exposed to the great impact of the peg-top. Symmetry, though desirable, is not necessary for prolonged spinning; any imbalance tends to be offset by the renewal of spin by the whip. If we may judge from eighteenth-century prints, the whip-top attained great bulk and perhaps great weight, rivaling even the large tops cast with so much skill by the Malays. Conversely, the whip-top seems to have found favor in smaller sizes than the peg-top. The reason is not clear; perhaps as the peg-top became smaller (and lighter) the air resistance to its flight when cast may have made its flight erratic. Figure 46 shows the smallest commercial* whip-top I have spun.

Worldwide distribution of the whip-top is found; the incidence is greatest in Europe, the Americas, and northeastern

* Dr. Wilson showed me smaller tops made by himself.

Figure 45. Whip-tops. (a) English top (based on Wagner); (b) Cottbus, Germany; (c) Antwerp, Belgium; (d) Zaandam, Holland; (e) Arapahoe Indian, Wyoming, U.S.; (f) Korea. Tops (b-f) are late nineteenth-century and bear University of Pennsylvania Museum numbers 21322, 21326, 21323, 36980, 17622, respectively.

a

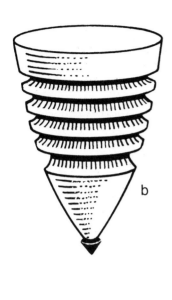

b

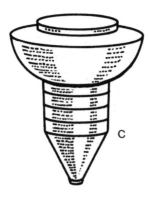

c

d

e

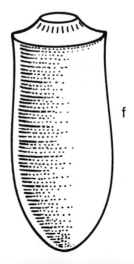

f

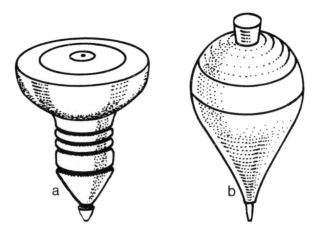

Figure 46. Small tops. (a) whip-top, 7.5 grams (University of Pennsylvania Museum number 21326); (b) South American peg-top, 11.5 grams (courtesy of the late J. W. Wilson).

Asia. It is less common in Africa, India, and southeast Asia; it is almost absent in some Pacific Island cultures. In modern America, the whip-top has almost disappeared from use.

THE WHIP

Almost all writers agree that the eelskin was the preferred material for the whip. But why? How the skin was prepared is not told, and we can only infer that the adjunct to a child's plaything would be an inexpensive, untanned skin. If untanned, the whip must have had attributes of suppleness and resistance to cracking. Old prints do not agree on the length of the lash, nor even upon the width and number of lashes. There is general agreement, however, that the lash(es) should be set upon a stock of about the same length.

Although the Europeans seem to have preferred eelskin, more primitive cultures in America and Asia used a wide variety of materials for whips: tendons, woven textile cords, and strips of skin (the latter with little processing). We have tried a number of modern fibers, including a waxed cotton line. The failure of some of these whips is not believed a function of the material. Figure 47 shows whips.

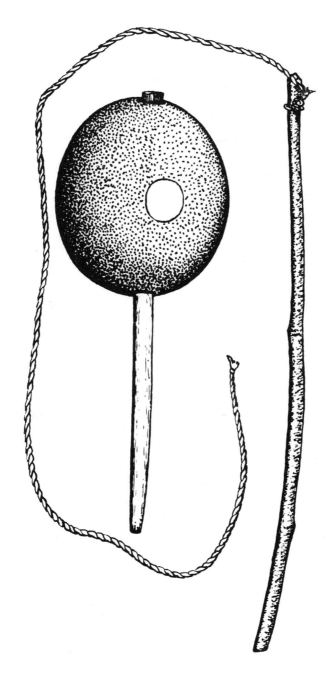

Figure 47a. Whips and whip-tops (based on Collins and Culin).

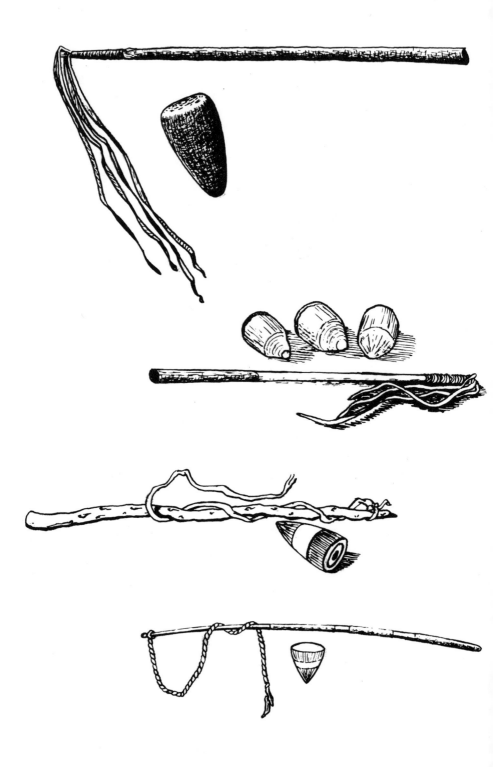

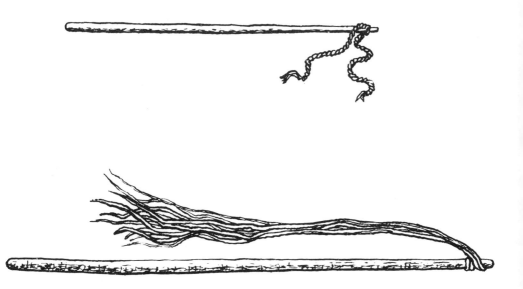

Figure 47b. Old and young join in whipping tops. Different types of tops in wood and stone are also illustrated (based on Reed).

Figure 10 shows children whipping tops, and this picture is confirmed by numerous descriptions of the sport (see also Figure 48). But the directions given by these writers are scanty. For the ambitious reader, the self-taught teacher herewith offers an exercise:

Hold the top in the left hand, bearing point to the right. Place the free end of the lash upon the side of the top slightly more than halfway above the mid-height. Take two or three turns of the lash about the top, winding in a clockwise direction. Still grasping the top with the left hand, rest the bearing point of the top upon the ground, and steady the top in an upright position with the left middle finger. Use the thumb and first finger to retain the lash in place. The grip of the right hand is now shifted to the stock, and the right arm is extended out and back to give a brisk pull upon the stock. Continue to support the top with the left hand, but release the lash at the onset of the pull. The top will spin in place with little tendency to drift.

The stock is now swung nearly parallel with the ground and at a distance from the top estimated to make possible envelopment of the body of the top with one or two turns of the lash. This is done with a single smooth motion that changes to a backward pull on the stock. The lash should take its turns around the body (or upper part) of the top. If the tapered end is engaged, there is a tendency to lift the top from the ground. This lifting is spectacular, but not to be sought by the novice. The frequency of lashing depends upon circumstances, but a single spinning action may have a duration of five seconds (seldom less) and this is an adequate interval to pose the arm for a renewed stroke. The above instructions apply to a wooden top about two inches high.

There is a recurring association of whip-tops with regions having severe winters—perhaps because hard, smooth ice is an excellent surface for the play. If one replaces the hockey puck

Figure 48 (a-f). Whip-tops of another century as shown in the art and writing of the times; (a) illuminated detail from *Roman d'Alexandre,* 1344.

(b, c) prints from nineteenth-century children's books (based
on Tuer).

WHIPPING TOPS

Whip top! Whip top!
Turn about and never stop!
Monday's top will spin away,
Tuesday's top will sing all day,
Wednesday's top is never slow,
Thursday's top to sleep will go,
Friday's top will dance about,
Saturday's top will tire you out!
Whip top! Whip top!
Spin around and never stop!

(d) poem from *Country Things*, by Alison Uttley.

(e, f) early prints (based on Daiken).

with a whip-top and provides whips instead of hockey sticks, a robust game can be imagined. Unorganized play could become a melee.

Occasional social significance has sometimes been attributed to the whip-top. Writers have suggested that the parish whip-top (Figure 49) was provided by the parish less with intent to give a healthful exercise than to keep excess animal spirits channeled into harmless pursuits. Note, too, the plea for equality of the sexes given in Figure 4(a):

> This is good exercise, and we know no reason why girls should not use it, in moderation, as well as boys; for, when they have been working with a needle for a long time in cold weather, the exercise will tend much to promote their health.

This pious declaration, circa 1800, might have carried more weight had it been illustrated with the depiction of former days shown in Figure 4(b). The tides of liberation rise and fall with uneven force. Manifestly, top-spinning was approved for both sexes in classical Greece; it is exceptional to find its association with women and girls in later European cultures, although the popularity of diavolo (pp. 171-79) attracted many women players. The Pacific island and Southeast Asian peoples had no uniform permissiveness; sometimes top-spinning was a wholly male sport, sometimes girls entered into its play; adult women seldom seem to have participated in any major way.

The top has not been an effective part of the arsenal of the caricaturist for over a century and it is not likely to come into favor again except upon the wave of a popular fad such as attended the yo-yo when ridicule was poked at political opponents (Figures 60, 61). A sharp note is seen in the cartoon by Cruikshank, which captures the discomfiture of Napoleon after Leipzig, and takes the victor's privilege of representing the

Figure 49. Perhaps the parish, or "town," top (based on Brand).

Figure 50. " The Corsican Top in Full Spin," caricature by
Cruikshank, 1814.

defeated enemy in a ridiculous attitude. Figure 50 shows the
hapless, dismembered Bonaparte as a whip-top treated with con-
tumely by the whip wielders. This was 1814, and marked the
end of ten years in which, more often than not, Napoleon held
the whip hand.

TYPE 5   THE BUZZER

Classical scholars have used the terms whizzer, magic wheel,
and rhombus interchangeably and sometimes loosely to denote
the buzzer (Figure 51). There have been misgivings in assigning
the title of top to some objects. The commonest concept of a
top is a spinning object supported at one point only. But the
gyroscope has a wheel whose axle is supported at two points,
and the motion of a projectile fired from a gun is that of a
top although there is no point of support. The inclusion of the
buzzer can be justified on the basis of premises associated with
the top: human interest in motion, the presence of a major axis,
and use as a toy. This top is simple and cheap. The origin is

lost in antiquity, but almost every culture has had the toy. Figure 52 shows an example from classical times and one from a primitive people of much later times. The top seems to have affinity with the fiber-spinning whorl in that both impose tension and torsion on fibers, and take advantage of the momentum of a whirling mass—in the top there results a bidirectional motion; in the fiber-spinning, there is smooth rotation given to the spindle and a more uniform stranding of the fibers.

The device is made from a disc, plate, or wheel through which strands pass. New Guinea natives with a Stone Age culture used a shell as the rotor; the Eskimo may prefer a leather disc; the European child may like a button. Wood, ivory, or bone will serve. The universality is real, and if the construction is often of non-durable material, this is perfectly understandable; the simplest material readiest to hand is sufficient. The strands passing through the rotor are twisted and untwisted, being alternately relaxed and placed in tension by torsion. The resulting spin is pleasing to the eye, and is often accompanied by a buzzing or humming sound. If the periphery of the rotor is serrated, the noise may be enhanced.

The reversible, pulsating motion is akin to the constrained, supported top shown in Figure 30. There seems to be a psychological effect and perhaps a physical one attending manipulation of the top. The sequence of pull-relaxation on the cord takes on the tempo of the pulse or breathing; the buzz is sonorous, lulling. By anchoring the cords at one end, the player then needs but one hand to operate the toy; native ingenuity saw that it could be done with no hands simply by looping the cords over the knees. The exhibitionist could use two or more tops simultaneously.

Figures 53–56 depict classical scenes with the top. The person holding the toy is often a woman or immature male. The significance of the object is debatable; our opinion is that the mild humming noise (note that most of the wheels have irregular rims) accompanied the voice of the player. No specimen of the wheel has survived and the construction material is unknown. The toy is usually found in a scene of affluence or Olympians.

The buzzer has a safe future, so much is in its favor! Materials are everywhere at hand; little skill in creation or operation is needed; and the results are satisfying.

Figure 51. Buzzer; common button and cord.

Figure 52. Buzzers. (a) Classical "magic wheel"; ceramic decoration; note the irregular outer edge of wheel (based on Deubner); (b) primitive African toy (based on Traore).

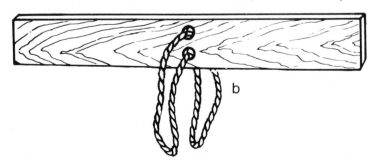

Figure 53. Magic wheel, and detail (based on Panofka).

Figure 54. Magic wheels. (a) from Leningrad (St. Petersburg); (b) based on Panofka.

Figure 55. Decoration on back of bronze Etruscan mirror (based on Gerhard).

Figure 56. Magic wheel in British Museum (based on C. H. Smith and Dumont and Chaplain).

TYPE 6   THE YO-YO

This toy (Figure 57), like the second variety of the supported-top, belongs to a class that might be called recuperative. As a result of the original impulse given it to unwind the cord, there is imparted a momentum sufficient to reverse the direction of rotation. The simplest manner of spinning the top is to take several turns of the cord about the waist (axis) of the top, hold the free end of the cord, and drop the top or throw it toward the ground. The cord unwinds and the top is rotated about its axis. As the top falls the extent of the cord, it is of course prevented from dropping further, but its kinetic energy manifests itself as inertia, and the top continues to rotate and appears to climb the string, winding the cord on the waist. It will not have enough energy to rise to its original position and hence will fail

98

to rewind completely. Friction of the cord upon the sides of the spool and the resistance of the air account for this loss of energy. Accordingly, the spinner must move his end of the string downward so that in effect the top continues to spin in space at about the same distance from the floor and re-winds the string completely. At this point, a quick upward movement of the hand starts the cord to unwind, but because of inertia, the top as a

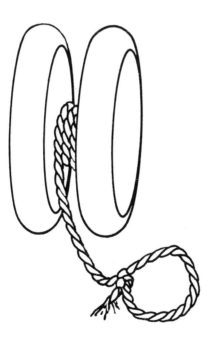

Figure 57. Modern plastic yo-yo.

Figure 58. Classical scenes on two sides of a ceramic yo-yo (based on Benndorf).

whole is lifted. Then the top falls, the string continues to unwind, and the process is repeated.

The recuperative principle of the yo-yo has been used by primitive peoples in the supported-top. Hindsight and knowledge of both types can be used to argue derivation from one or the other. Certainly both display ingenuity to a high degree.

The artistic Greeks have given us evidence of its use. The upper part of Figure 58 has caused discussion among archaeologists. The top shown there has resemblance in shape and cross-section to the modern, conventional yo-yo. The object is ceramic, and its fragility as a child's toy is evident. Some persons have thought it was a spool to receive thread. The artistry and

Figure 59a. Two sides of a classical Greek ceramic yo-yo (Metropolitan Museum of Art).

skill lavished in making the spool seem to argue that this was a prized possession of an affluent family. But would this shape and material be so chosen? We are doubtful; wooden spools with a broader winding surface would seem a more likely choice (as indeed they are today). Another group has seen the object as representing an ornamental feature—part of the house furnishings. Set in the wall, it could be used to support cords on which

draperies were hung, or simply as an ornament. It is a logical explanation, but fragility is a serious defect in a moveable ornament. Further, if the ornament is used as a permanent architectural detail, why is it adorned on both faces? Our prejudices prevail; the object is a toy, and specifically, a top. Votive in nature perhaps, but yet a workable yo-yo. (See also Figure 59 a, b).

Figure 59b. Vase decoration (based on Benndorf).

The lower portion of Figure 58 shows a vase decoration which may be dated to about 500 B.C. Despite controversy as to whether the person portrayed holds a top, it may be said that if another artist had intended to show a yo-yo, he could hardly have changed the picture. Above, we said that ceramic tops may have been votive and intended as an offering, not as a toy. A top intended as a toy would probably be made of wood for durability. In any event, the ceramic top appears operable, albeit great care must be taken. Preller, the archaeologist, was doubtful that the object was a top because there was no hole in the shaft between the discs to receive the cord. But no hole is necessary; simply tying the cord securely to the shaft enables the top to be spun in the usual manner.

In the classification of tops and in this section, we have referred to the yo-yo. No ascription to advertising is intended; further, we think the name is rightly in the public domain. Note that Preller in 1852 applies the term *Joujou* to a toy of this nature.

No one knows when the yo-yo appeared in modern Europe. Larousse's *Grand Dictionnaire* (Paris, 1866) states the top was invented in 1791 and that a single establishment in Paris made twenty-five thousand of the toys in a short term. But Meyer's *Lexikon* (Leipzig, 1927) calls the toy *Kletterkreisel,* and further says it was known to the Greeks and brought to Paris from the Orient in 1790. Others say the top was brought to France from Peking by returning missionaries. The French minister of state, Henri-Leonard Jean Baptiste-Bertin (1720–1792), was an amateur collector of Chinese curiosities, and his attention to the toy may have given it excellent publicity. The yo-yo's early names— *émigrette, émigrant, émigré*—seem to date from 1789 when the rolling of feudal heads caused great numbers of nobles to flee France. The children of these families carried with them the toy then greatly in vogue. The yo-yo also acquired the name of *de Coblenz,* presumably from the large number of French refugees in that city who had brought the toy with them. Figures 60 * and 61 † catch the spirit of the times.

Men, women, and children have often been seized by the craze of yo-yo play. The makers of the toy cautioned that it was best used outdoors, in the interest of safety to persons and breakable objects. Around 1790, it replaced the *bilboquet* (Figure 62a) in favor, though the *bilboquet* is still to be seen in Latin America. It consists of a ball and a cup. The skillful user of this toy can give the handle a sharp upward jerk and catch the ball in the cup. This writer never attained proficiency, but, in trying, he afforded much amusement to a scornful seven-year-old. Bouasse [41] describes an interesting toy (Figure 62b) that combines the yo-yo and the *bilboquet*.

The overwhelming popularity of the yo-yo in the nineteenth century led to the formation of clubs that could compete in performing intricate and difficult tricks with the toy. From France, the yo-yo swept through the rest of Europe. In England it was called bandilor or traveling top; in Greece, it was the disc. About a century later, a recurrence of the fad attracted so much attention that a Persian newspaper carried an angry article denouncing the dangerous toy, imported from the United States, as "an example of a time-consuming and immoral novelty." Apparently things have not changed much and the wire services, on February 13, 1969, gave American newspaper readers an eye-catching story of a 15-inch, 4-pound yo-yo successfully manipulated from a 10th-floor window. I have been assured that the motive behind the experiment was fun, not

---

* André Boniface Louis Mirabeau, nicknamed "Barrel" Mirabeau, emigrated about 1790 and raised a legion of counterrevolutionaries that was to bear his name.

† I am indebted to Dr. R. Simard who commented on this caricature by saying that the aristocrats were being ridiculed by showing the royalist followers wielding ineffectual weapons. The "Air de Malborough" is a doubtful allusion to the Duke of Marlborough. However, the name Malbrouck is also found in Chansons de Gestes of the 11th to 14th centuries and "Malbrouck s'en va't-en guerre" is an 18th-century ditty sung to the tune of "For he's a jolly good fellow" and "We won't get home until morning" in Britain.

▶

Figure 60. Mirabeau lampooned (based on Allemagne).

Mirabeau Chef d'une Légion,
de l'Armée noire et jaune en grand uniforme.

Figure 61. Le Jeu de l'Émigrette (based on Allemagne).

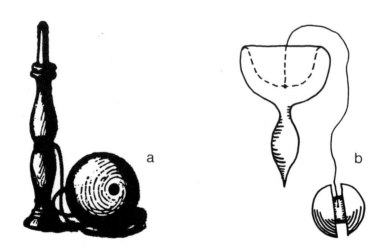

Figure 62. Bilboquets. (a) cup and ball (based on Allemagne); (b) modified as yo-yo (based on Bouasse).

science. Yo-yo play has long been considered a prime example of moronic activity; this description, however, is not likely to diminish its popularity, and this toy has passed into the repertory of adult and professional spinners. The simultaneous use of two or more tops by a skilled performer is truly amazing, both hands doing evolutions that would defy the usual solo spinner.

BIBLIOGRAPHICAL REFERENCES

Twirler:	28, 70, 90, 112, 166, 174, 176, 187, 190, 207, 250, 291, 322, 323, 347
Supported top and Bracket:	19, 25, 39, 84, 94, 174, 187, 200, 209, 214, 246, 253, 300, 322, 347
Peg-top:	28, 36, 66, 67, 70, 94, 106, 117, 123, 131, 174, 214, 215, 224, 246, 276, 299, 320, 327, 352
Whip-top:	2, 25, 26, 27, 28, 32, 43, 61, 66, 67, 73, 90, 94, 102, 106, 117, 154, 171, 174, 179, 187, 188, 198, 201, 224, 246, 259, 264, 327, 348, 353
Buzzer:	18, 61, 70, 91, 102, 166, 209, 222, 256, 323, 347, 353
Yo-yo:	4, 22, 25, 28, 29, 66, 102, 123, 131, 134, 224, 285, 317, 340, 347, 363, 364

CHAPTER FOUR

GAMES PLAYED WITH TOPS

THE DISTINCTION between the terms toy and game as used here places weight on the latter where emulation or competition exists. The toy is essentially a pastime to amuse the single player (the buzzer and yo-yo are examples). The purist will point out correctly that the objects used in some games may themselves be toys. The top has wandered happily into both categories, but in this chapter we will note games based on several classes of tops.

The spinner or twirler top lends itself to low-keyed play. It is cheap, simple to use, and durable. Two important games were invented early for this kind of top; they are still in use, and well suited for two or more players.

In the first variant, each player has a certain number of spinners and a playing area of his own. At a given signal, the players start their pieces spinning. (A piece that falls dead may be picked up and restarted.) The first player to have all his pieces spinning simultaneously is the winner.

In the second variant, the players start their pieces in motion

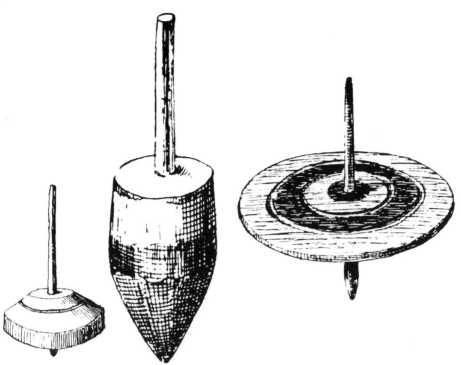

Figure 63. Eskimo spinners (based on Culin).

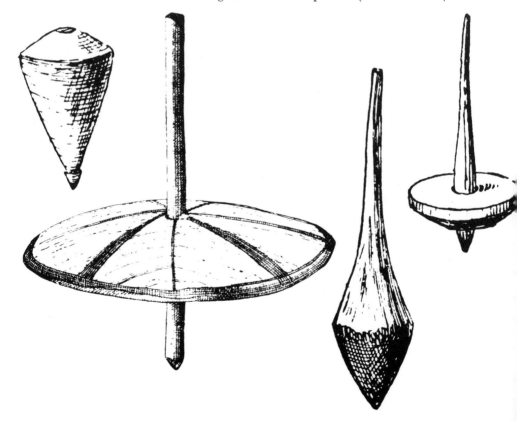

at a given signal. At a second signal, the player with the largest number of pieces spinning is the winner. In a variation of this play, said to be used by the Eskimos, one spins a single top, rushes out the door, makes a circuit of the house, and re-enters before the top stops spinning. Some of the large twirlers made in non-European cultures are so well balanced that the reported Eskimo game gains credence. Figure 63 pictures a number of small Eskimo tops.

When a twirler slowly ceases to rotate, it becomes unbalanced and falls to rest. The point of the body lying uppermost is wholly random; this fact is the basis for the use of the top as a decision-maker, that is, leaving to chance the answer to a question. The first use of the twirler for this purpose is lost in the distant past but many variants have kept their freshness to the present day.

The top may be used for determining moves in board games (such as "race-horse" or variants of Parcheesi) and, strangely, for fortune-telling. In one Oriental usage, which must have been psychologically convincing—if not pleasing—the player was permitted to make his own entries upon the blank faces of the top. Here was a way to make Fortune stand and deliver; obviously the player should submit more readily to ill-luck prescribed by himself because he and Fortune had been in accord.

There are also versions of the teetotum, such as the top with four faces, and the characters P and T alternating on each face. This is a simplified version of "put and take." The appearance of P or T as the top comes to rest requires the addition to or the subtraction from the pot by a fixed amount, usually equal to the individual's original ante. Exhaustion of the pool signals termination of the game or renewal upon the original terms.

Freeman noted that the term teetotum is sometimes applied to balancing toys (Figure 64) where the center of gravity of the system a-b-a is below the pivot point c; Crabtree would call this a top. A nineteenth-century book describes a marbles game in which a conventional teetotum, bearing numbers instead of letters, is set spinning and a player then shoots or snaps a marble at the top to upset it. If successful, the player receives a number

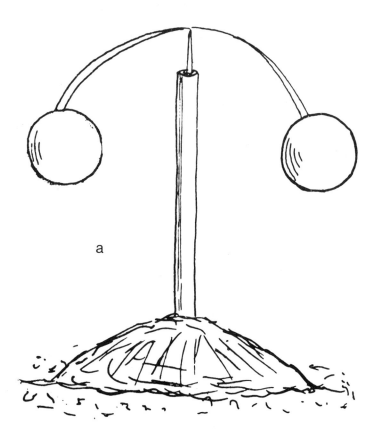

a

Figure 64. Gyrostats. (a) based on Griaule; (b) based on Perry.

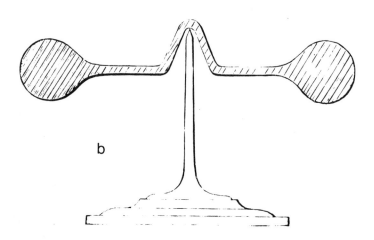

b

of marbles equal to the figure uppermost as the top comes to rest.

The supported-top finds a place in such games as a diminutive version of skittles. Competing players set their own tops in motion in a common spinning area, using the rotating top to knock out of action smaller or lighter objects in the area. Another form of play is when the contestants try to move their spinning tops through paths or channels counter to opponents' efforts.

The peg-top does not seem to have existed—or at least was not described—in classical times, although many more primitive cultures had developed this toy. It has given the world more kinds of play than all other forms of tops, and Western Europe was especially rich in games which employed the peg-top. It is the only top that has had its games described at length in European literature. In such games, the spinning of the top is accomplished by the owner in a single, concentrated effort with the objective either of accuracy in casting or long duration of spinning.

Spinning within a target area falls in the first category. This play is particularly satisfactory. Cock, in describing such games in the Netherlands, shows the manifold variants where the target area may be marked by crossed lines. Figure 65 shows examples of common targets. The best shot is upon the intersection; the next best is upon a line, and is judged by the distance from the intersection. The poorest shots touch no line. A version given by Marran, where two or more players compete, uses a target area divided into segments of unequal value. The scoring is wholly determined by the segment in which a top "dies" and rolls to a stop.

Displacement of objects from the target area by a spinning top also falls within the category of casting the top with accuracy. This game rewards the skillful with the object that has been placed at hazard within the target area. The stipulation that the top cast at the objects must spin is the key to successful play and must be enforced scrupulously in adult competition. Gomme described a British version called Gully. A player puts a

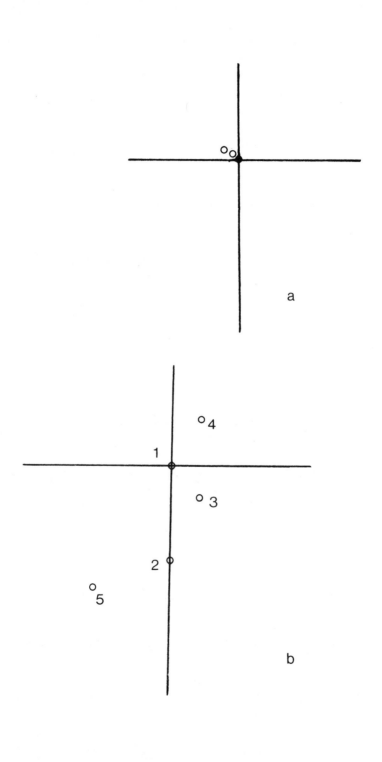

a

b

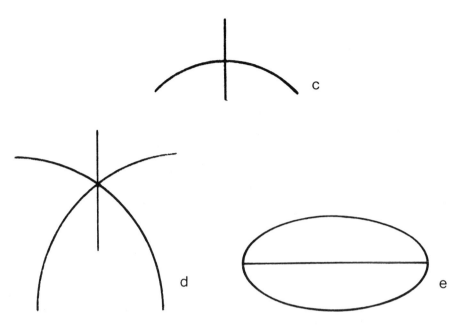

Figure 65. Common targets. In (a) or (b) rules would govern the degree of credit for landing upon lines, or nearest to lines. In (c, d, e) rules would usually apportion credit for landing within segments of playing area rather than by proximity to lines.

top on the ground at some distance from a hole (hence the Gully) or other designated spot. The second player casts his top with intent to push the recumbent first top to the hole. If a miss results, the player can pick up his yet-spinning top between the fingers and onto his palm. He then drops the top to strike a glancing blow upon the opponent's top to move the latter toward the gully. This might be a good two-handed game; it combines skill in casting, deftness in moving the spinning top to the palm of the hand, and a nice judgment of time and space in dropping the top. Another version stipulates that if the second effort fails, the aggressor's top must go into the ring as a target. Gomme's detail of the penalties attached to losing in this variant and in "Hoatie," or "Hots," is just as savage as any from Asia.

The game of "Hoatie", or "Hots", demanded that the target top be struck by the caster's top; in the event of failure to obtain a hit, the aggressor's top could be seized and deliberately mutilated.

A more civilized contest involving displacement is, in fact, Oriental and is depicted in Figure 103, item 34, and Figure 109. The scenes show peg-tops spinning on an inclined surface. This surface may be matting, a blanket, or other semi-yielding material draped over a tub or box. When tops are cast to spin on the surface, they naturally migrate toward the low portion of the surface. They may be expected to collide and perhaps one will be knocked off this area. A remaining spinning top is declared the victor. This is a game for one, two, or three persons, and differs from its European counterpart of "peg-in-the-ring" in that there is no intent to inflict injury on an opponent's top, and contact of the tops with each other is practically assured on the sagging surface. In our observation of peg-in-the-ring contests there has been only infrequent contact of the cast competing tops. The conditions of the Japanese game lend themselves to gambling. Culin noted that in the event both tops are knocked from the matting, the top initially thrown is credited with the advantage, having spun longer. The game's name, *bai* or *bei*, derives from the shell used as a top, Filling the shell with wax, sand, or the like was common usage to increase the top's weight.

It is in the Malaysian states of Kelantan and Trengganu on the east coast touching the South China Sea that top spinning has the status of adult sport. It is played with such zest and skill that a description of the tops and of one version of competition is warranted.

The tops from these states are turned from sound, close-grained wood (Figure 66). All are spun with a cord like any peg-top. Although the top may have a peg, this feature is not prominent, and in some tops it may project hardly a quarter-inch from the body. It is a bearing surface, and obviously not made to injure an opponent. At least a half dozen turns of the cord are required to give good performance. It is said that some

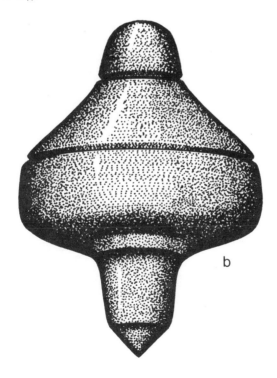

Figure 66 (a-d). Malaysian peg-tops (University of Pennsylvania Museum numbers 16188, 16184, 16187, 16189 respectively).

a

b

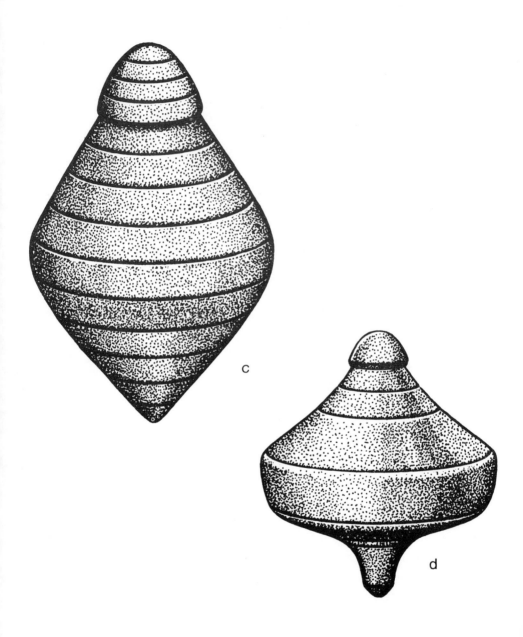

c

d

tops have spun for twenty minutes (presumably on a hard, smooth surface). The spinning tops can be tossed from person to person by looping the cord about the body of the top and may be caught upon the flat surface of a paddle resembling a cricket player's bat.

In 1966 we witnessed the following contest which involved strictly adult competition between players of nearby *kampongs* (villages). Each person had three tops, usually carried in a net bag. All players exhibited utmost decorum and intensity of purpose. The visiting players paid their respects to the local headman as soon as they arrived.

The area in which the competition took place was astonishing. The only preparation of the ground was to clear away brush and stones. The surface was fairly level, but no effort was made to smooth it (Figures 67 and 68). One "court" was considered slightly muddy, and a brushfire was lighted to dry out the soil. The tops were about six inches in diameter, two inches thick, and weighed about two pounds. The cord initially wound on the top for several turns was about one-eighth-inch diameter (resembling cord sometimes used on venetian blinds). Several turns were taken with another cord of about one-quarter-inch diameter, spliced to the first. A loop in the end of the heavier cord was slipped over the wrist, and several wraps of excess rope were taken about the hand. At every turn, the cord was drawn very taut on the top.

The contest began with the defending team casting their tops to spin on the prepared area. Three tops were set in motion as a group, hardly separated from one another (Figure 68). The delivery in casting resembled somewhat that of a baseball pitcher; it was performed with great force and precision (Figure 67). The forward movement of the arm was followed by a whip-like return and a tremendous crack of the cord. Despite the unpromising appearance of the ground, the tops spun smoothly and without change of position. A member of the offense then cast his top, attempting to strike a specified opponent's top and knock it from the formation. This player is allowed some latitude in positioning himself for the throw. So far, the game

Figure 67. Top-spinning contest Kelantan, Malaysia, 1966.
Delivery of top (1 of 3) by defending team.

►

Figure 68. Top-spinning contest, Kelantan, Malaysia, 1966.
Member of offense positioned for attack on defender's tops.

might be said to resemble the contests once common in Europe. The Malaysian requirements were that the elimination of a defensive top by a knockout was valid only if the attacker's top remained spinning, and further, if it did not touch any but the specified top. We saw no cast that seemed intended to injure the opponent; casts that were ineffective were greeted with derision. Prestige depends entirely upon ability to cast the attacking top accurately and in a manner to remain spinning. The successful elimination of the defender's final top was accompanied by a bit of gloating. The attacker deftly looped a cord about his still-spinning top and transferred the top to the palm of his hand, while he invited the recognition of the onlookers. At this point, the roles of the teams were reversed, and play resumed. Three casts are made by the attacker; points are awarded for successful elimination of defender's tops; penalty points are given for improper attack.

There were no women in the audience, and only a few boys (who were not allowed part in the play). It was understood that women and children were neither prohibited nor invited to the games, which seem only for adult male diversion. Small wagers are said to be laid on the outcome of the contests. We saw no rancor: minor differences were adjusted by the headman without challenge. The whole affair had the appearance of an enjoyable amateur athletic contest. The writer was permitted to spin a top (with moderate success) but the language barrier was too great for active participation, even if he had possessed the requisite skill.

Haji Mubin Sheppard of Kuala Lumpur makes note of some of the variants which appear in this type of contest:

The order of play assigned to the teams, either defensive or attacking, may be determined by an initial casting of tops; the offensive is taken by that team whose top remains spinning longest.

After play has started, and in the event that the attacker has not displaced all the defender's tops, the top that remains spinning longest is awarded a point. (The defense throws its tops in a manner to stress duration of spinning and tightness of formation; the attacker is more concerned with casting the top to displace the defender.) If the attacker fails to hit the defender's top, his team automatically loses the round and becomes the defending team.

The peg-top as an adjunct to duration-of-spinning contests has probably reached its highest development in the hinterlands of Malaysia. I am indebted to Dr. Sheppard for his generous assistance in portraying what may be a waning pastime. Here is his description of the trial of a top to be used for duration contests:

"The winding of the rope on the top (whose weight was about twelve pounds) was a major operation. The rope was over one-half-inch thick and was made of thirty strands of thin cord; its length was over four yards. The spinner knotted one end around a porch pillar, and pulled the top and rope with all his might as he wound the top. Two turns of the rope were taken about the wrist, and the top was raised to shoulder height while it was grasped much as would a discus thrower. There is a fierce "crack" as the rope whips back and the spinning top is seen, seemingly without motion, on the hard ground. A colleague darts forward to the top and scoops it up with a *Chokok*, a spade-shaped wooden object. In a single swift motion, he transfers the top to a *Lopok* which has a shallow, metal, saucer-like surface and set upon a short section of bamboo stuck upright in the ground."

On the metal surface, the top may spin for a prolonged period; the record as known to Dr. Sheppard is one hundred minutes. In contests of spinning duration, the player performing the transfer is equal in importance to the spinner.

Figures 69 to 75 show scenes in which the large top is used.

The whip-top seems to have had very wide distribution as an adjunct to play and games. Classical Greece, Western Europe, Asia, and aboriginal North America provide examples of the strenuous nature of top-whipping, sometimes the prelude to a melee.

Whip-top play presents several competitive forms. In its simplest aspect, two individuals set their tops in motion and try

Figure 69. Spinning the large Malaysian top (adapted from Peters). The first step is to impose the cord as tightly as possible.

Figure 70. The top may be poised as shown or sometimes is held like a discus.

Figure 71. Delivery.

Figure 72. The cord is then retracted in a swift motion.

Figure 73. The rapidly rotating top is about to be picked up with the wooden *Chokok*.

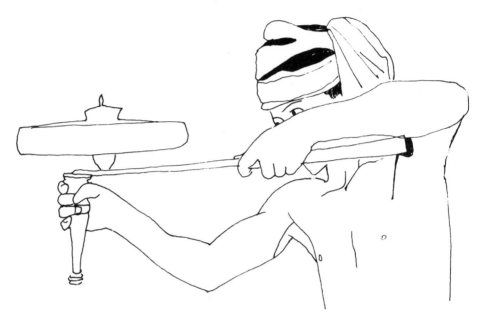

Figure 74. The top, spinning on the *Chokok,* is transferred to the *Lopok* held in the right hand.

Figure 75. The *Lopok* serves as a pedestal, and the top may spin there for many minutes.

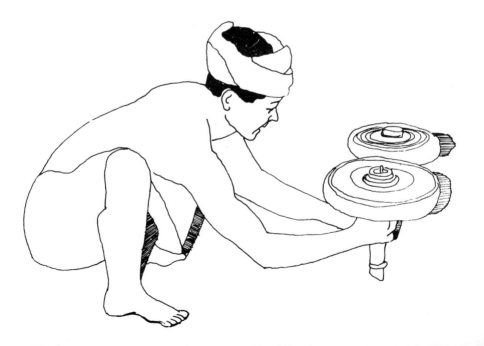

to outlast the opponent in duration of successful whipping. A more vigorous form of the sport is where each player tries to cause his top to cross a line. Another variant of the game permits two or more players of the same team to perform the whipping (Figure 49). Finally, two opposing teams can use a single top and attempt to drive the top into a designated area. In this latter variant, the resemblance to lacrosse or hockey is plain.

Literature of Elizabethan England provides extraordinary evidence of whip-top spinning as a schoolboy's sport. That Shakespeare should speak of tops no less than four times argues that the practice of spinning tops was a common pastime in his day. From his plays come: ". . . played truant, and whipped top" (*Merry Wives of Windsor*, V. i. 27) an obvious reference to a schoolboy; and ". . . not big enough to bear a school-boy's top" (*Winter's Tale*, II. i. 103). The schoolboy's top would be a trifling object and the allusion is one of derision. Still another mention in Shakespeare is ". . . turned me about with his fingers and thumb, as one would set up a top" (*Coriolanus*, I. ix. 24), and ". . . turn o' the toe like a parish-top" (*Twelfth Night*, I. iii. 44). Schmidt says that this is a large top kept in a parish for public exercise. Elsewhere it is spoken of as a means of keeping idle hands out of trouble, and of stirring the blood on cold nights. No authentic parish top seems to have survived, but sketches purporting to portray the object suggest that it was large (perhaps eight inches tall) and weighed two pounds or more (Figure 49). To keep this top in motion over the uneven surface of a courtyard would indeed stir the blood. Some scholars have discounted the allusion to the parish top as a jest. However, it has been suggested that rivalries between towns or parishes in the form of athletics or sports could include contests with whipped tops (resembling hockey or lacrosse in causing the object to encroach on opponents' part of the field). The town or parish top would be a valued community possession both for practice and in actual competition.

Finally in Shakespeare we have ". . . as one would set up

a top" (*Coriolanus*, IV. v. 161). This refers to the whip-top. The common practice is to take a couple of turns of the whiplash about the top and to hold the top lightly in an upright position on the ground. The lash is then withdrawn in a swift lateral motion of the whip-stock, the fingers supporting the top being simultaneously lifted from the top. This "setting up" of the top involves some skill.

And an official attitude toward top-spinning may be sensed from a description of Harrow School founded almost four centuries ago in the reign of Elizabeth I. The notable, though not noble, John Lyon established Harrow School which was to take its place, along with Eton and Rugby, among England's distinguished public schools. Set forth by the benefactor were "Orders, Statutes and Rules" dated January 18, 1591, a significant part of which follows: ". . . The scholars shall not be permitted to play, except upon Thursday only sometimes when the weather is fine, and upon Saturday, or half-holidays after prayer. And their play shall be to drive the top, to toss a handball, to run, or to shoot, and none other." Now here is a thicket of punctuated phrases, and a stern disciplinarian might well curtail play and easily be within the letter of the statute. More than enough to start a full-scale demonstration on any campus today. We can only surmise that the pupils of that day got very little parental backing for relaxing discipline.

The words "to drive a top" meaning to play with a whip-top, brings to mind the Dutch name for the object, *driftol*. No doubt the play was praiseworthy as inexpensive and a means of stirring the blood. Harrow was no exception to the meager heating of sixteenth-century living quarters.

The words "to shoot" presumably referred to archery, a sport consistent with the yeoman background of the early Lyon's young beneficiaries. Probably the schoolboys of the time did not consider themselves harshly treated, and Harrow's name derives neither from a daunting of the spirit nor from agriculture.

There is no evidence that Elizabethan schoolboys knew forms

of the top other than the whip-top. But voyages of exploration and commerce would soon bring new contacts with strange tops and would also create astonishment that some very primitive people had tops "such as we have at home."

The buzzer is essentially a toy for solitary performance, and the only games we have seen children play with this device seemed of spontaneous invention. The first variant consists of setting the top in rapid rotation and then allowing it to touch edgewise to the ground. The strings are held slackly, allowing the wheel to advance for a considerable distance. The player whose top runs farthest on the ground is the winner.

The second game is played by two or more persons each with a buzzer, who place their tops in rotation and then connect one end of the looped cord to the looped end of another player's cord, each player retaining hold upon his respective remaining loop. The demands upon coordination are great in order to continue the spinning of the two wheels.

The yo-yo lends itself to a player's individual ability rather than group performance. In this it resembles the buzzer and the supported-top. An exception might be when a group of players attempt to manipulate their yo-yos through a sequence of pre-stated stunts.

Gleanings from an Age of Innocence and

Wood Block Printing

A review of library holdings related to games, toys and play show a remarkable number of pictures depicting top-spinning of young children. This suggests that the top held its own as one of the favorite toys of the eighteenth and nineteenth centuries. The artists' compositions (Figures 76–80) often show a skill never quite approached by this author. The dimensions and shapes of the toys are usually credible; perhaps the artists once were top-spinners.

BIBLIOGRAPHICAL REFERENCES

50, 70, 87-90, 108, 145, 152, 174, 187, 204, 207, 250-252, 296, 306, 322, 325, 327, 332, 343, 360

►

Figure 76 (a-c). Eighteenth- and nineteenth-century woodblock prints (based on Cats, Wagner, and Comenius respectively).

a

b

C

Figure 77. Wood-block prints showing peg-tops (based on Daiken and W.P.A. respectively).

Figure 78. Wood-block prints showing whip-tops (based on Daiken).

a

Tom kept learning his book,
And cheerful did look,
  Of the fool's cap no longer in fear;
Got his master's good word,
Was head scholar preferr'd,
  And the above fine medal to wear.

He had a whip and a top,
Bought for him at the shop,
  And a great many playthings beside,
And his father with joy,
Bid him keep a good boy,
  And he should have a horse for to
    ride.

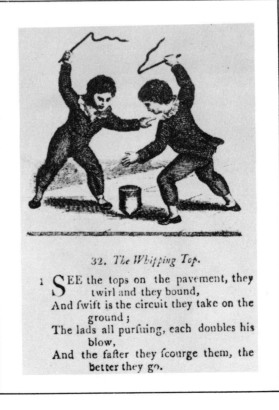

32. *The Whipping Top.*

1 SEE the tops on the pavement, they
    twirl and they bound,
  And swift is the circuit they take on the
    ground;
  The lads all pursuing, each doubles his
    blow,
  And the faster they scourge them, the
    better they go.

b

THE HUMMING BALL

Augustina. Willingly—This game only requires a little practice—look well—you see that I first hold these two little sticks tied together by this small cord, keeping them at a little distance, that the ball may keep its balance in the bending of the cord. I raise my hands alternately, to impress it by the motion; and I elevate my right hand much higher, by slight jerks, which makes it turn. I gradually quicken this motion, to increase its rapidity, that the ball may keep its balance, which accelerates its movements, as you may perceive, and causes it to hum. This is the effect of the air which enters by these little holes; the noise augments in proportion as its celerity increases, and almost resembles that of the harmonica.— Come, try in your turn.

C

Figure 79 (a-c). Wood-block prints showing whip-tops and diavolo play. (a) based on Devries; (b, c) based on Tuer.

141

PEG TOP

I knew a little boy who nearly lost one of his toes by a violent blow from one of these tops: the peg entered his foot, and if immediate care had not been taken it might have been dangerous. Surely then peg top is hardly safe. It often happens that by wetting the string too much it so fastens around the top as not easily to be disengaged: and when this is the case the bystanders are in great danger of receiving hurt, as many little boys can assert the truth of, who have gotten hurt by standing too near the ring. Many think too little of danger when any favourite amusement is at hand. But what a pity it is that young folks will not take warning by the misfortunes of others but go on the old way till the like befall themselves.

Figure 80. Wood-block prints showing peg-tops (based on Tuer).

· C H A P T E R   F I V E ·

MATERIALS

STONE WOULD seem to be a most unlikely choice of material for tops because wood has been plentiful for all peoples, except perhaps the Eskimo Indians (who sometimes use ivory or bone). There is, however, a recurring mention of mineral matter in tops. Some of these oddities will be discussed.

Heinrich Schliemann's spinner (Figure 3) found at Troy may be about three thousand years old. Today, we may accept it as a top, but wonder whether it was made then as a toy (far more expensive than its wooden counterpart) or was intended as a votive offering. A votive object is a gift dedicated to the honor of the god worshipped; to this day, there are devout persons who present a cherished article in gratitude to a saint. Customs have varied; sometimes the offering is a cheap item and is simply symbolic; at times the gift is costly. The Trojan trifle survived the millennia because it was ceramic.

In classical times, some ceramic tops were given such costly decoration that we can hardly suppose these breakable items were used as toys. Yet some of them (particularly yo-yos) certainly could be used if given reasonable care, and even if intended as a votive offering, the construction represents as much attention to operability as a cheaper version intended specifically as a plaything. (See Figures 7 and 58 of a whip-top and a yo-yo.)

Among the more primitive societies of the nineteenth century, there were found stone tops which were not votive yet unquestionably they were used as tops. The weight of some has been estimated at two pounds. If the top is symmetrical, the axis well centered, and care is given to the bearing point, such a top can be a spectacular performer in the skilled hands of the owner. It seems certain that these people when making a heavy top realized that the top would spin longer under the initial impulse. The elaborate baskets used to carry the tops are evidence of the value of the toy.

The Ojibway Indians of North America reportedly used water-worn stones as tops, but no accurate description has been found. In view of Crabtree's report of the use of celts as tops (Figure 12) there is a slight possibility that these were the tops of those Indians. Figures 81, 82, and 83 show other stone tops, including a terra-cotta whip-top (Figure 82e) dating to the Roman occupation of Britain.

The New World presents some notable examples. An accumulation of over eighty stone tops from a pre-Columbian site in

Figure 81. Stone tops. (a) whip-top, New Zealand (based on Edge-Partington); (b, c, d) teetotums from New Guinea, spun between palms of hands. Item (b) has its own carrying basket indicating the value given it by its owner.

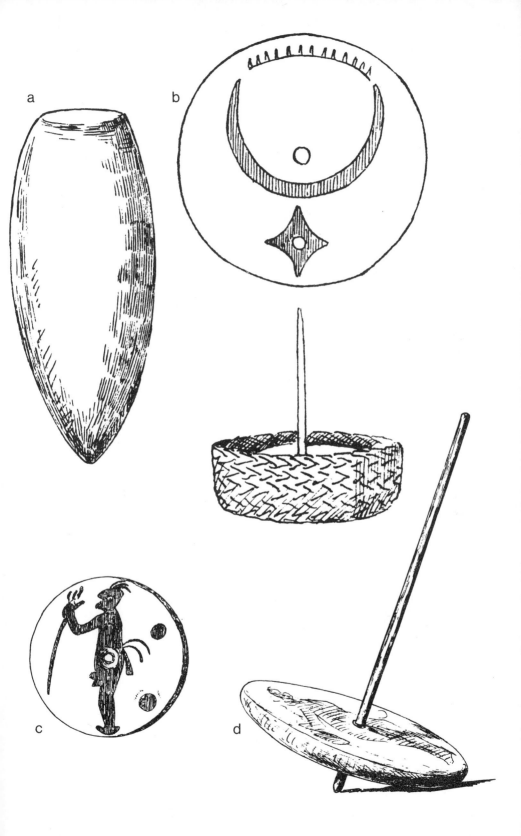

a

b

c

d

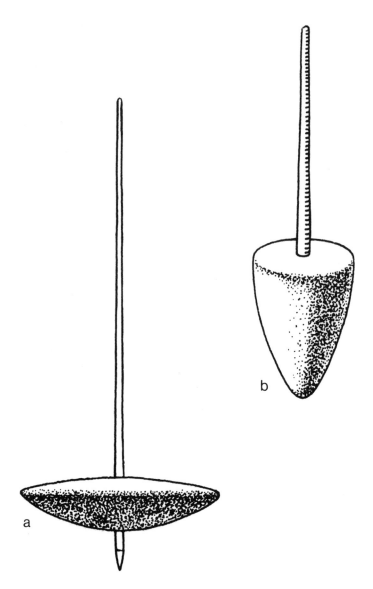

Figure 82. (a-c) teetotums made from mineral matter (based on Reed, Best, Haddon); (d-f) ceramic whip-tops (based on British Museum, Cuming, Allemagne).

c

d

e

f

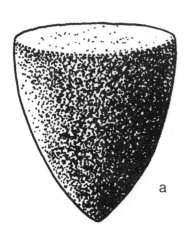

a

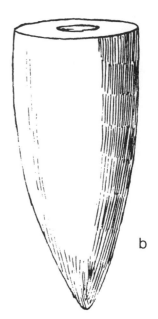

b

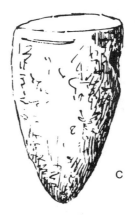

c

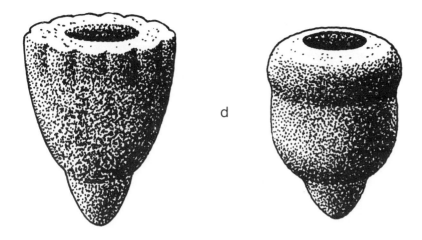

d

Figure 83. Stone tops. (a) whip-top of coarse coral, Oki-
nawa, late nineteenth century (University of Pennsylvania
Museum number 21422); (b) teetotum (based on Edge-
Partington); (c) whip-top of pumice, New Zealand (based
on Edge-Partington); (d) stone tops from Tiahanaco, Bolivia, have a distinct circumferential depression, perhaps to
receive cord. (Max Uhle expedition, 1895, University of
Pennsylvania Museum number 36077.)

Bolivia has been viewed. The specimens range from one inch
to three inches in height, and from smooth and symmetrical in
finish to rough, crude, and distinctly ill-formed in appearance.
With two exceptions, they are or could be whip-tops. The exceptions (Figure 83d) show a pronounced circumferential depression about half an inch from the lower end. We did not
spin these objects with a cord, but are confident they would
respond to the usual techniques of peg-top spinning.

Here is a problem for the researcher: If the objects are accepted as archaeological specimens and as tops, then the peg-
top may gain new stature as having an ancient origin, and the
ascription of the whip-top in the New World to European ex-
plorers and colonists must be restated. It is the writer's opinion
that the top has been invented independently many times.

SEEDS, NUTS, AND FRUIT USED AS TOPS

Hardly a writer on the juvenile aspect of tops has failed to mention that the child of the unlettered savage uses a berry or an acorn as a top. This might seem to emphasize the trivial nature of the toy, and to reinforce the idea of the undeveloped mind of the savage. What is seldom mentioned is the discovery that a slender stem, spike, or thorn if used as an axis is the real substance of such tops and that this is a complex development. Before that, the acorn, for instance, is only an infrequent or accidental top. If acorns are kicked at random, the flight of one of them may take a spinning motion; the nut moves in an orderly fashion like a rifle bullet.

There is no way of knowing when the top, born of a seed or fruit and an imposed axis, was first invented; the perishable nature of the material precludes this. Tops made by the Ojibway Indians observed by Kohl in the vicinity of Lake Superior, and the Maori of New Zealand using coconuts, could be no better than the tools available for piercing the nuts permitted. Although the end use may have been as a child's toy, the fashioning was likely to be that of an adult.

Some of today's American children who perhaps will never see a conventional top may nevertheless be taught to combine a toothpick and a berry into a top and thus produce the toy that has provided fun for a thousand generations. Figures 84 and 85 display tops made from seeds and nuts.

►

Figure 84. Tops from the vegetable kingdom. (a) recuperative top from Jamaica, twentieth century, *Entada scandens* (courtesy of the late J. W. Wilson); (b) made from nut, New Hebrides (based on Edge-Partington); (c) recuperative top, Africa (based on Béart).

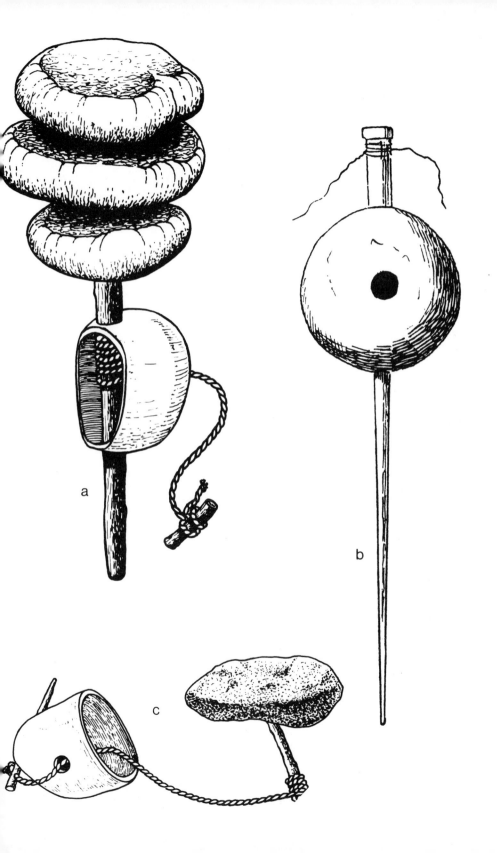

a

b

c

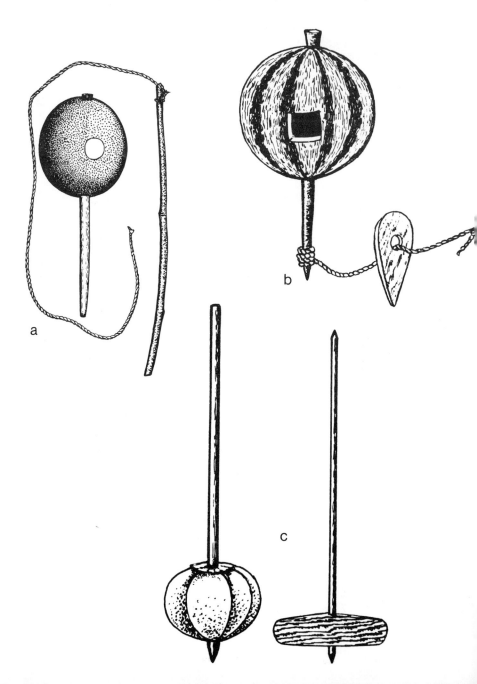

Figure 85. Tops from the vegetable kingdom. (a) whip-top, Liberia (based on Collins); (b) recuperative tops from French Equatorial Africa (based on Béart); (c) Mer (based on Haddon); (d) coconut shell (based on Edge-Partington); (e, f) spinners of nuts and berries from Africa (based on Griaule); (g, h) twirlers (based on Griaule).

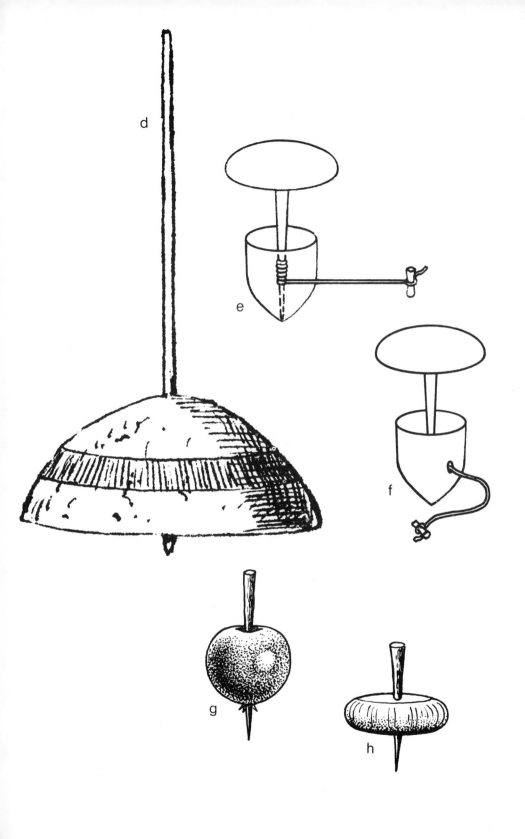

SHELLS

It is reported that univalve shells have been used as tops, particularly in Eastern Asia, and that wax or lead has been used to make the tops heavier. We have not had such a toy, but did experiment with a murex filled with sand. The bearing point was very crudely rounded. Limited skill and the choice of material yielded only fair results in spinning with a whip. Later, a much larger shell from a Chinese collection was seen in which a metallic, conical cap was fitted over the point of the shell. The object was not used as a top, but the method of closure seemed good.

Shells are a potentially plentiful source of material for tops and would have invited trial by peoples adjacent to the seacoast. Because such tops would be easily damaged by impact, they would be less suitable as peg-tops. It might be presumed that anyone talented enough to fit a peg to a shell would already have grasped the superiority of a material with uniform density that could be shaped as desired, and would choose wood. But the shell may be a contender for the title of the earliest top, and the reader will recall that the accidental movement of some bivalve shell may have revealed to early man a motion that has henceforth fascinated him.

PLASTICS

We had developed a fine contempt for the use of plastics as construction material for tops, and were puzzled and finally impressed by their recurring appearance in the twentieth century. First there was the twirler (Figure 86), actually a "giveaway" in a package of popcorn. Its weight was less than two grams and the symmetry and balance of this top allowed this toy to spin readily for a duration of twenty seconds or more. Its cost? Perhaps a tenth of a cent!

Now, there have appeared all types of plastic tops. Plastic yo-yos, diavolos, and so forth, are common, and some are well made.

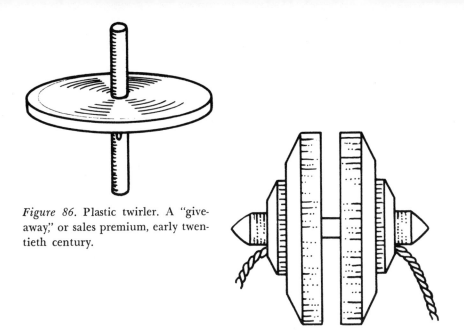

Figure 86. Plastic twirler. A "give-away," or sales premium, early twentieth century.

Figure 87. Plastic combination top for use as a double-ended peg-top or as a yo-yo; modified to serve as a buzzer; mid-twentieth century.

In most instances the plastic tops will withstand harsher treatment than their wooden counterparts and are, of course, much lighter in weight, a great advantage in aerial tops.

We were intrigued by a plastic top (Figure 87) which performed well as a yo-yo and spun smoothly as a peg-top when cast with a sideways motion as was recommended for item (b) in Figure 32. Then we drilled a hole on either side of the axis to receive a cord and behold, an effective buzzer resulted. No invention is claimed—probably the object could be readily modified into a supported-in-starting top as well.

BIBLIOGRAPHICAL REFERENCES

Ceramic and stone: 8, 25, 51, 52, 71, 74, 84, 89, 112, 116, 134, 167, 178, 199, 224, 231, 291, 323

Seeds, nuts, shells: 8, 25, 31, 51, 52, 71, 74, 90, 116, 167, 178, 179, 224, 292, 300, 323

CHAPTER SIX

DERIVATIONS

THERE IS a surprising vitality to tops; age-old forms disappear and reappear; favor is won and lost, and sometimes the world is given a new top. In this section we are going to discuss some longtime favorites and one top new enough to have occasioned technical writings almost immediately upon its appearance.

THE SPRING-TOP

Figure 88 shows two spring-tops. They are to be considered twirlers (Type 1) because a spring gives a sharp, sudden twist to the top's stem usually made with the fingers. The device consists of a top and a spring-holder. The spring-holder (Figure 88c) is set on the stem of the top and is twisted with the right hand. Nibs or ears on the holder engage recesses on the upper surface of the top. The spring is thereby coiled and can be triggered by pushing the stem protruding from the holder.

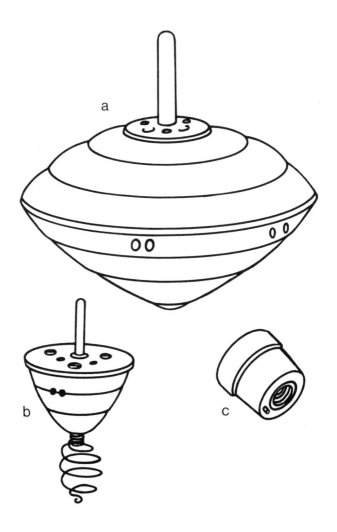

Figure 88. (a, b) spring-tops; and (c) a spring-holder.

The released body falls spinning to the floor. The operation is sure and the spinner is satisfied. This top was once a great favorite with children unable or unwilling to spin conventional tops. It was a product of nineteenth-century technology, but has gradually deteriorated in quality. Few remain in operable condition; the spring mechanism is the first to fail and repairs are difficult.

Referring to Figure 88(a) and Figure 19, item 25, it is evident that these could readily be spun with a bracket in the manner of other supported-in-starting tops (Type 2). The top pictured in Figure 88(b) is intended to be ejected from the holder several feet above the floor. A vigorous bouncing action ensues.

Figure 19, item 26 is described as having a spring in the holder (below) to perform the ejection and rotation of the top itself.

THE DISC AND THE FRISBEE

Primitive man was (and is) aware of objects that can be given a flight quite different from those familiar objects such as fruits or pebbles. The unusual objects are "scaled" rather than hurled; the fingers and wrist are more involved. If the object is thrown upward and away from the player, it returns, more or less, to him. The plane of the object remains nearly parallel to the line of flight and the axis of rotation is perpendicular to the trajectory. Such objects have been further developed in recent centuries and Figure 89 shows the characteristics of two specimens: a modern Frisbee and an older disc derived from India. (We shall discuss the Sikh disc in Chapter 7 under weapons.)

One of the delights of the Frisbee is that it can be thrown horizontally in a nearly straight line for a considerable distance. No precise tests have been made, but it is believed that the initial velocity that must be given to obtain a flat trajectory is

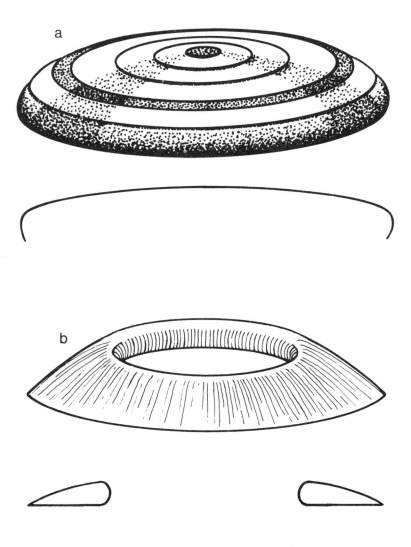

Figure 89. (a) Frisbee (plastic) and (b) Sikh disc (steel).

much lower than if a ball were thrown. The Frisbee can afford pleasure and exercise to two or more players who may be unaware that they are using a modification of a primitive top.

TOPS SET IN MOTION BY A THRUSTING MOTION

Of the body motions imparted by the player there are four: pull, throw, twist, and thrust. This last was probably born during the nineteenth century, when the spiral thread or screw was incorporated into the top's mechanism. Figure 90 (a) and (c) shows tops about five inches in diameter and six inches high, made of brightly decorated tin with a number of holes in their shells. They are so constructed that a downward thrust on a plunger–only the knob handle is visible in (a) and (c)–which moves in a spiral path down a threaded core imparts a rotary motion to the body of the top. At the completion of the downward stroke, the plunger is disengaged and drawn up for another stroke. In the meantime, momentum has kept the top in motion, and succeeding strokes have some cumulative effect. The speed of the rotor increases as the tempo of thrusting increases until the top has achieved enough speed so that it can stand unsupported on its point, as would a common top when spinning. And if the thrusting is continued and increased in rate, the top will emit a distinct hum because the air flowing past the holes in the shell sets the edges of the metal and the enclosed air into vibration.

This top has been a great favorite with adults (who have the strength to operate it) and presumably with small children because it gives pleasure to their elders. Many of these tops were well-constructed and could stand much abuse. Within recent years, on visits to toy stores to purchase tops, I have found only this type available; stocks of all other kinds being unreplenished

a

Figure 90. Tops set in motion by thrusting action. (a) and (c) are so-called musical tops. Knob handles are seen; spiral thread is concealed. (b) and (d) are set in motion by combination of thrust on follower and a pull on loop of spiral thread (after J.J.).

b

c

d

"until top season." One toy presented all the aspects of the conventional musical top, but had, in addition, a train of small cars that moved on a platform within the body of the top itself. The lily has been gilded.

As an alternative to the thrusting action, musical tops have been made to be spun by a string as for any restrained top (see Figure 91). Tops such as these are at an obvious disadvantage in that motion (and sound) cannot be sustained after the initial impulse.

If one looks at items (b) and (d) in Figure 90, there is seen an interesting variant to items (c) and (a). The top is operated when one hand exerts a pulling action on the loop of the helical rod while the other hand pushes or thrusts upon a follower. Obviously the elements of item (d) may be incorporated into a top with audio properties.

This use of a thrusting action and a spiral path found a new application when the direction of the thrust was reversed, that is, applied upwardly. Instead of a bulbous body, the rotor became light, slender, and propeller-like in form (Figure 19, item 44). The pitch of the blades gave a sufficient bite on the air so that the propeller could be placed in vertical flight. A youngster could exert enough thrusting force (no longer a cumulative effort) to move the rotor upon the threaded shaft at considerable speed. We have seen plastic models whose flight was spectacular, soaring in a loop perhaps a hundred fifty feet in extent, and returning very close to the operator. Metallic propellers could be placed in flight, and altitudes of several hundred feet were possible; men were already thinking in terms of "flying machines." This top has had remarkable favor, but it is now competing with toy rockets that afford ten times the altitude at ten times the expense. Yet I do not think that even in its heyday the aerial top could be expected to compete with its musical cousin, which had observable sound, sight, and motion. The motion of the aerial top is too distant to be followed easily.

The examples of the musical top and the aerial top which derive their motion from force exerted in a spiral path have their counterpart in the rifled gun whose projectile has a

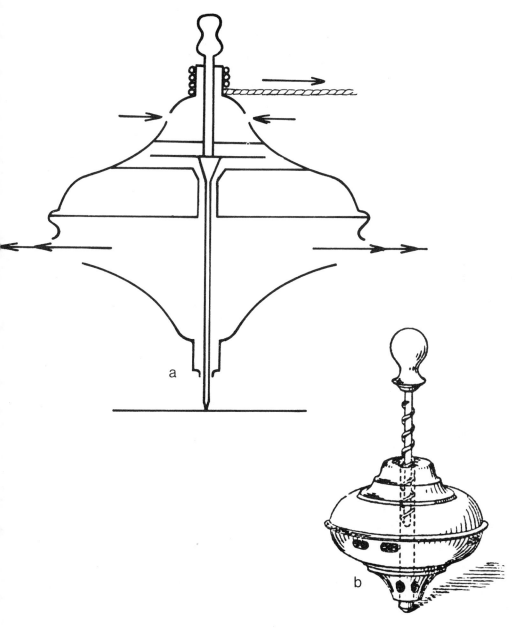

Figure 91. Musical tops. (a) cross-section of light metal supported-top (based on Bouasse); (b) plunger-type with helical axis.

dominant translatory motion but the spiral path imparted by the gun's rifling serves to keep the projectile in a controlled line-of-flight. Inevitably, an explosive charge has been used to give motion to the top as a toy.

We have met some frustration in researching the audio effects of tops; museum specimens plainly marked or catalogued as "humming tops" would not hum under ordinary conditions. This was particularly true of wooden specimens. The labels on the objects might more properly read ". . . having the approximate shape of humming-top X." Top X is found to have pro-

Figure 92. Humming-tops, late nineteenth-century (University of Pennsylvania Museum numbers 20275, 21316). (a) made from gourd, Northeast Queensland; (b) turned wood, Cottbus, Germany. The bracket (c) is suitable, but not original to the tops.

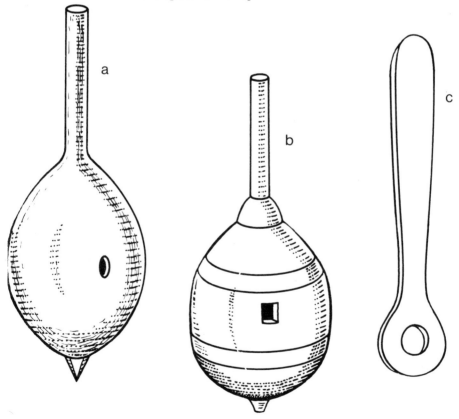

jections or indentations that produce the sound effect. Figures 92 and 93 show humming-tops. The imaginative natives of some South Pacific islands made tops that emitted low-pitched sounds and encouraged the spinners to join in song. A modern diavolo that had several perforations in its cones produced a high hum (or a low whine), which could be sustained. Buzzers with serrated wheels are capable of sounds with a wide range of pitch; the pitch is a function of the speed of rotation. It is the author's opinion that the buzzer often shown in classical scenes sometimes provided a low-keyed accompaniment to the human voice.

Figure 93. Humming-tops. (a) European (based on Wagner); (b) solid wood with metal point; ¼" × ¾" hole on bias (University of Pennsylvania Museum number 29-191-287b); (c) Maldive Islands, late nineteenth century (University of Pennsylvania number 16192).

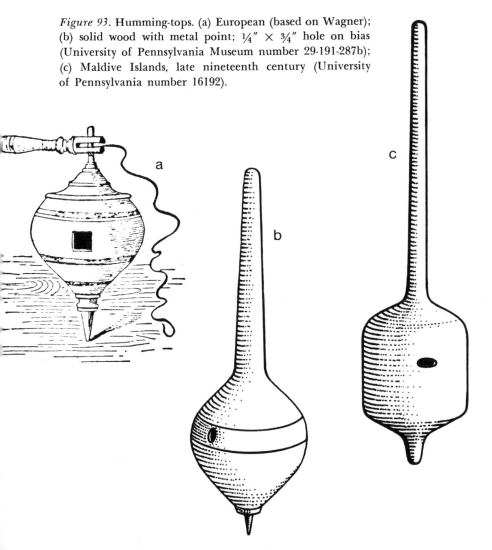

SOME EXOTIC TOPS

Early pioneers with tops, such as Serson, Troughton, and Fleuriais and, indeed, every inventor trying to adapt the gyroscope to man's needs, pondered how to keep a top rotating at constant high speed. To analyze the top's action mathematically, one had to postulate a constant speed. This is no longer a problem; a gyroscope can be designed to run at any chosen speed, and its rate of rotation need not vary one percent. It may be driven by an electric motor.

And within this century a new set of devices that operate at high rotational speed has evolved. The designers seem to be in a race for the highest rotating rate, recalling past efforts to approach absolute zero in temperature. Attainment was the thing; application would come later.

Probably the first and chief beneficiaries of very high rotational-speed devices were those who sought to separate substances through centrifugal force. The effectiveness of a centrifuge increases as the square of the rate of rotation—a potent incentive to increase speed. However, the disruptive effect of this force on the machine itself increases, too, as the dimensions of the machine are increased along the diameter. As a result, the emphasis is upon small diameter, high speed, machines. How to provide a bearing or the lubrication for the bearing was something to be tackled in turn.

For the reader who finds it difficult to accept the idea of a centrifuge as a top because the centrifuge is not point-supported, we can say that a similar doubt assailed us when we looked at the supported-top. We can take refuge in the nomenclature used by the scientists evolving the ultra-fast machines. Their designation is unmistakable—a top. In our opinion the rotor is a top whether confined by its bracket or not.

Briefly, the constant-speed electric motor to turn the rotor of the gyroscope was proposed almost a century ago. Twenty years later, a disc of mica mounted on a bearing received the passage of static electricity to spin this rotor. Less than thirty years after that, speeds of 10,000 to 35,000 revolutions per minute were being attained with iron rotors in a magnetic field. And near the turn of this century, a rotor, magnetically suspended, was spun at 100,000 rpm by pressure of light. There is a tenuous kinship between these machines and the top in Figure 19, item 24. In this latter top, the impulse comes from a stream of air directed through the spool. Experimenters with navigational tops, too, tried a controlled air blast as a driving force; of course the impulse would be continuous.

Ever since Troughton, experimenters have been aware of the retarding effect of air surrounding the spinning top, and have sought to reduce air pressure in the chamber containing the top. The ultra-high-speed top described above operated in a vacuum comparable to the atmosphere of the earth at an altitude of more than one hundred miles.

DIAVOLO

This familiar object (Figure 94) does not seem to have as long an ancestry or as wide a distribution as most tops. The name itself is uncertain: sometimes "diabolo," perhaps applied

Figure 94. Diagrammatic features of the diavolo top (based on Crabtree).

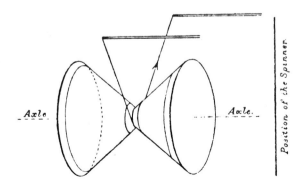

by frustrated beginners, often "diavolo," implying two sections in flight. Another source suggests the name diabolo is derived from the Greek *diaballo*, "to throw," acceptable perhaps because one of the important acts of play with the toy is the throwing of the spool back and forth between players. The Greek word also carries the meaning "to slander," whence diabolos as slanderous used in the sense of the slanderer, the devil. The sport of manipulating this top might well have originated in the Orient as part of a juggler's repertory. McClintock says the Chinese have played the game for centuries under the name of "Kouen-Gen."

Another source reports that Lord Macartney had seen it in China during his ambassadorship. Upon his return in 1794, the toy came into vogue in London and from there traveled to Paris. The source adds: "And that was all the profit Europe had from the ambassadorship of Lord Macartney." King Edward IV of England (c. 1470) and Louis XIV of France (c. 1700) also enjoyed this top.

The top seems to have acquired the name diabolo about 1812. It is certain that at its highest popularity there were organizations of ardent players in Paris, such as Le Diabolo Club, Le Cambio Club, Le Rochette, Le Devil Club, and Club du Jeu de Diable. Play is best done outdoors for the sake of breakable objects (but see Figure 95). While the vast majority of spinners share with the present author a pride simply in keeping a diavolo in motion, the aficionados recognize several important variations. Allemagne carries depictions (Figure 96) of players and equipment. The routines include the common rotation of the top on its cord; a maneuver whereby the spinning top balances and is made to "walk" along the baton; tossing the rapidly rotating top and making it appear to climb the cord; and, finally, using the batons themselves to spin the top.

In Figure 97 the top is caught by the crossed batons; a trick where the tossed top is caught on the hooked end of the baton (we have never seen this difficult feat performed); the spinning top is tossed in the air and is caught as it falls on sagging cord;

Comment on apprend à jouer au diable.
D'APRÈS UNE GRAVURE DE MODES DU PREMIER EMPIRE.

Figure 95. Diavolo, aptly captioned (based on Allemagne).

Figure 96. Above and right: Routines of the skilled diavolo player, part 1 (based on Allemagne).

L'ascension à corde tendue

Jean s'en va comme il est venu.

Le grand Equilibre du Croissant

Le saut Périlleux

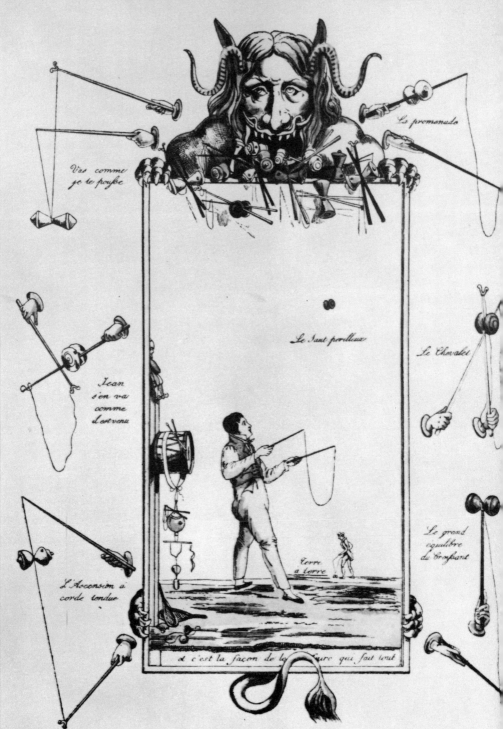

LA MANIÈRE DE JOUER AU DIABLE.

Le Goût du Jour. N.º 19

and a spinning top is made to "walk" along the ground much as a yo-yo can be made to do.

The French are said to have added a hooked end to one of batons (Figures 96, 97), which made greater variety of manipulation possible. The French have been credited, too, with modifying the basic shape from that of two cones conjoined at the apex to that of two rounded objects, a dumbbell shape, with intent to make play more difficult (Figure 98a). Be that as it may, the toy has been found in Africa with an almost cylindrical shape that probably offers a still greater challenge (Figure 98b). The author's experience has been confined to the double-cone type, which is well balanced and provides a narrow groove for the string.

Culin says that the Chinese version of diavolo, called "devil on two sticks," used a very large top.* But sticks are not essential.

This top is well adapted to solo amusement and to strenuous team play as an adult diversion. The size and weight of the top vary from that of a thread-spool to as large as a man could readily toss and catch. Although the shape has changed many times, it has always retained its symmetry and center of gravity at the midpoint. Like the whip-top, the diavolo is placed in motion and kept spinning by a cord. The cord, usually two to four feet long, is attached at its ends to wands (batons) held by the

---

* We were startled to find a wooden museum object shaped like the cone diavolo, and weighing perhaps two pounds. It seemed to confirm Culin's description, but the catalog identifies it as "an object for captive bears to play with." One wonders at the choice of shape.

◄

Figure 97. Routines of the skilled diavolo player, part 2 (based on Allemagne).

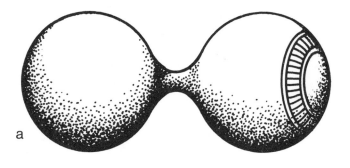

a

b

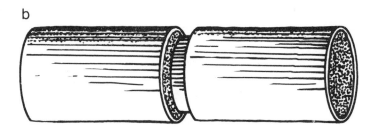

Figure 98. Diavolos. (a) French modification of cone shape;
(b) African (based on Griaule).

player. With the top resting on its side (in stable equilibrium) and the cord passing underneath the top at its waist, the player raises one wand higher than the other. The effect is to roll the spool away from the higher hand (although it cannot escape, being restrained by the segment of cord held by the lower hand). The spinning motion of the spool gives the top a measure of stability in a horizontal position just as the peg-top assumes a vertical position when spun. The more rapid the spin of the spool, the more stable the position.

If the spinner is deft, the top will have a high rate of rotation and the spool will be given an upward vertical displacement. As the top starts to descend, the player quickly reverses the relative position of his hands, bringing that which was lower to a higher level. The falling spool is caught and the lift-rotation is again imparted, and this action is continued at the will of the player. There is a continuous rotation of the spool in one direction, and the possibility of considerable imbalance of the spool. The instructions which usually accompany the toy point out: "If the spool tips downward toward the spinner, he moves the right-hand wand toward him. If the spool tips away from the player, move the left-hand away." To this we add a bit of experience: the initial practice is best performed over a bed; otherwise much clatter and stooping accompany one's efforts. To the serious student of the game, we recommend Ward.[351]

PLATE AND WAND

About the middle of this century there occurred a professional revival of a juggler's act ascribed to the Chinese. A plate or saucer is set in rapid motion upon the end of a slender stick or wand held vertically. There is usually a slight indentation on the lower surface of the saucer to receive the end of the wand. For best effects, the plate should not balance precisely on the

Figure 99. Plate and wand (based on Doolittle).

wand when at rest; a slight imbalance will cause the saucer to wobble alarmingly, but the rapid rotation will make the disc take a horizontal position. The skill of imparting this rapid rotation is almost lost upon the spectator; it is the loss of rotation and the erratic wobbling that catch the eye. The wobble imparts itself to the audience who share the seeming frantic haste and worry of the showman to keep the object safely turning. During the spinning of the top, the juggler may perform other acts of balance, litheness, or dexterity. Figure 99 shows a juggler in his act; an appreciative audience would certainly applaud the balancing of the plate upon the stick held in his mouth.

MAGIC OR SILHOUETTE TOPS

It is sometimes said that the approaching end of a biological species is heralded by bizarre forms, and, indeed, the close of the dinosaur era saw variants seemingly unable to survive. There have been times in the past century when tops changed for change's sake. The persistence of primitive forms may be due to their simple design and the availability of materials, even to children. And yet there is such an admirable wealth of new ideas that to disparage change is neither kind nor wise. Some of these ideas may have never got beyond a patent office model —the inventor risked his all, and lost to an unreceptive public. Mentioned and illustrated here are some that enjoyed fleeting popularity. In Germany, where many novelties seem to have originated, there was one called *der Zauberkreisel*, the magic top. Despite its many forms, it depended upon the principle of centrifugal force to extend some part of the top and thereby create a new silhouette which seems part of a larger revolving object. Figure 100 is representative. The wire form inserted in the center of the platform spins with the platform and creates the illusion of a solid. Varying degrees of stiffness or rigidity

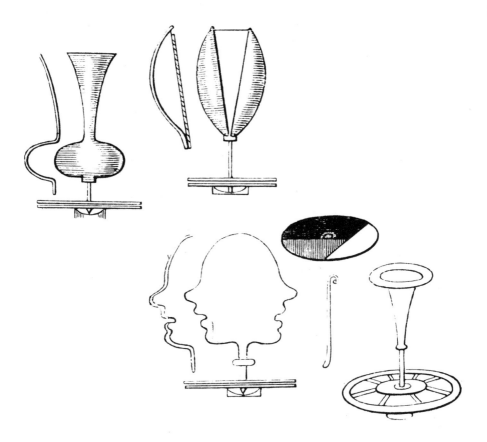

Figure 100. Zauberkreisel, or Magic Top (based on Wagner). The wire forms are inserted on the platform; when the platform revolves, the wire forms create the illusion of solid figures.

of the form allow different creations at different speeds (Figure 19, items 22 and 38).

The pirouetting doll (Figure 101) responded to the top's motion and extended her arms in a graceful manner. This response to centrifugal force is the same used in the governor of an engine, where the extension or deformation of an element at high speed serves to actuate a throttle, and thereby prevent the engine from going faster.

Figure 101. Pirouette doll may be spun as a twirler or with a bracket placed over stem of head (University of Pennsylvania Museum number 21301).

EAST ASIAN AND (PARTICULARLY) JAPANESE TOPS

This subject has been given a separate section, not only because of the recognized importance of East Asian tops, but also because of the persistence of the toy in Japan's culture and the astonishing variety of tops available there today. The Japanese themselves ascribe derivations of the top to neighboring Korea and China (Figure 102 and Figure 45, item f). The Chinese noted early that the rapidly revolving top seeks an upright position and maintains this against other forces.

In contrast to Europe, we see in the Orient two important factors in the development of tops and top-spinning: First, the spinning of tops was considered more than a child's pastime and became part of the performance of the showman—juggler, magician, or itinerant salesman gathering a little group of prospective customers—which necessitated tops made by a skilled artisan; second, a natural product, bamboo, provided material that was strong, hard, of medium weight, and round in section. Whereas other top makers might depend on the lathe for turning tops, the Oriental artisan found bamboo quite adaptable in its natural state. And where the top turned from a block of wood is of the same density throughout, a cross-section of a bamboo stalk at a node exhibits the properties of a flywheel with much of its mass near the perimeter.*

The distinctly cylindrical top (Figure 102) is commonly used as a so-called humming-top; its counterpart in other lands is usually derived from gourd-like materials (Figure 92a). Many Oriental tops tend to have an unusual stem length; this is practical only with bamboo and metal. A long-stemmed top of ordinary wood is likely to be injury-prone or to require unusual workmanship.

Peg-tops are preeminent in Southeastern Asia and Pacific island cultures, but the twirlers and supported-tops of the Orient seem to surpass those of other areas. Even if we were to dismiss Japanese peg-tops and whip-tops as being essentially no different than what the rest of the world has known, we could yet admire the rich variety of shapes and colors available today (Figures 103–107). Caution! Throughout accounts of Japanese tops, it has been difficult to differentiate † names, that is, what

---

* Of course a woodworker could turn cylindrical sections from a block of wood to give the equivalent of a bamboo stem, but hardly for a toy.

† The gracious assistance of Mr. Masaru Harada, Philadelphia, is acknowledged; deviations from locally accepted terms is my responsibility.

Figure 102. Humming-top. Chinese, bamboo, late nineteenth century; readily spun with bracket (University of Pennsylvania Museum number 21464).

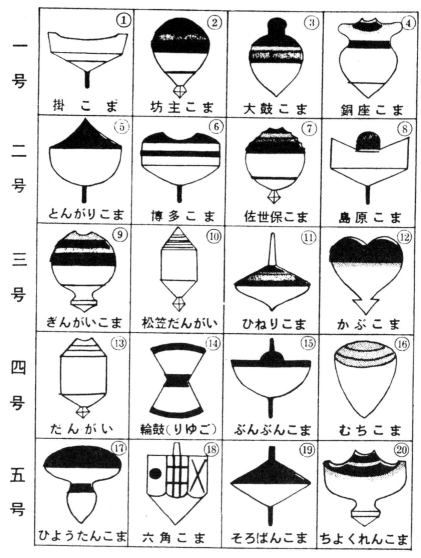

一号	掛こま ①	坊主こま ②	大鼓こま ③	銅座こま ④
二号	とんがりこま ⑤	博多こま ⑥	佐世保こま ⑦	島原こま ⑧
三号	ぎんがいこま ⑨	松笠だんがい ⑩	ひねりこま ⑪	かぶこま ⑫
四号	だんがい ⑬	輪鼓（りゆご）⑭	ぶんぶんこま ⑮	むちこま ⑯
五号	ひようたんこま ⑰	六角こま ⑱	そろばんこま ⑲	ちよくれんこま ⑳

1. *Kake*, i.e., seat-shaped supported-top
2. *Bozu*, bald peg-top
3. *Taiko*, drum peg-top
4. *Doza* (locality), peg-top
5. *Tongari*, pointed twirler
6. *Hakata* (province), supported-top
7. *Sasebo* (province), peg-top
8. *Shimabara* (province), supported-top
9. *Gingai* (province), peg-top
10. *Matsu kasa*, straw-hat peg-top
11. *Hineri*, twist twirler
12. *Kasu*, turnip peg-top
13. *Dangai*, straight side peg-top
14. *Riyugo*, drum cinched in middle diavolo
15. *Bun bun* (sound of top), supported-top
16. *Muchi*, whip-top
17. *Hiyotan*, gourd whip-top
18. *Rokuhaku* (hexagonal teetotum), twirler
19. *Soroban* (like disc of abacus), supported-top
20. *Chokuren*, peg-top

Figure 103. Contemporary Japanese tops. Yamamoto, Nagasaki; Numbers 1-20 (courtesy of the late J. W. Wilson).

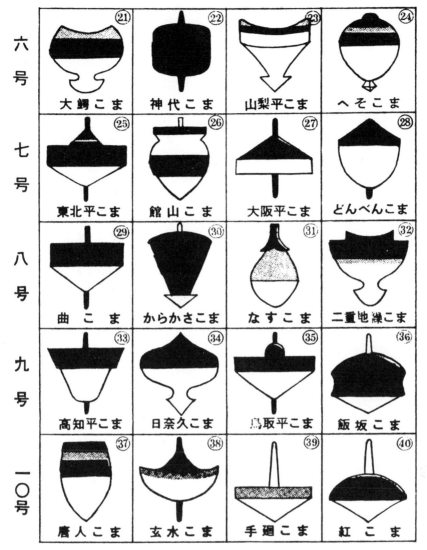

六号
七号
八号
九号
一〇号

㉑ 大鰐こま	㉒ 神代こま	㉓ 山梨平こま	㉔ へそこま
㉕ 東北平こま	㉖ 館山こま	㉗ 大阪平こま	㉘ どんべんこま
㉙ 曲 こ ま	㉚ からかさこま	㉛ なすこま	㉜ 二重地練こま
㉝ 高知平こま	㉞ 日奈久こま	㉟ 鳥取平こま	㊱ 飯坂こま
㊲ 唐人こま	㊳ 玄水こま	㊴ 手廻こま	㊵ 紅 こ ま

21. *Dai wani*, alligator peg-top
22. *Shin dai*, an early type twirler
23. *Yamanishi* (locality), peg-top
24. *Heso*, navel peg-top
25. *Tohokuhsi* (locality), supported-top
26. *Hirayama* (locality), peg-top
27. *Osaka* (locality), supported-top
28. *Don ben*, bowl and cover peg-top
29. *Kyoku*, supported top common with children
30. *Karakasa*, peg-top resembling partly folded umbrella when inverted

31. *Nasu*, eggplant
32. *Nijujikuru*, double scallop peg-top
33. *Tota hei* (locality), supported-top
34. *Hinaku* (locality), peg-top
35. *Totori hei* (locality), supported-top
36. *Hanzaka* (locality), twirler
37. *Tojin*, Chinese style whip-top
38. *Gensui* (family name), supported-top
39. *Temawashi*, hand-spun twirler
40. *Pink* (presumably color of top), twirler

The tops 1-40 of Figures 103 and 104 were examined but not spun by the author; the comment as to classification is based on other tops of the same approximate shape but varying in size.

Figure 104. Contemporary Japanese tops. Yamamoto, Nagasaki; Numbers 21-40 (courtesy of the late J. W. Wilson).

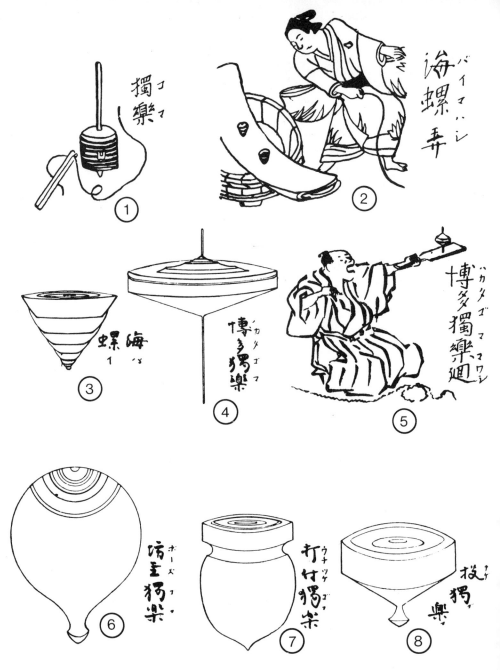

1. *Koma*, from the *Wa Kan san sai dzu e*.
2. *Bai mawashi*, conch-shell game. From the *Wa Kan san sai dzu e*.
3. *Bai*, conch-shell top.
4. *Hakata-goma*.
5. *Hakata-goma mawashi*, Hakata top-spinning.
6. *Bozu-goma*, priest-top.
7. *Uchi tsuke-goma*, striking-top.
8. *Nage-goma*, throwing-top.

Figure 105. Japanese tops, late nineteenth century; Group 1 (based on Culin).

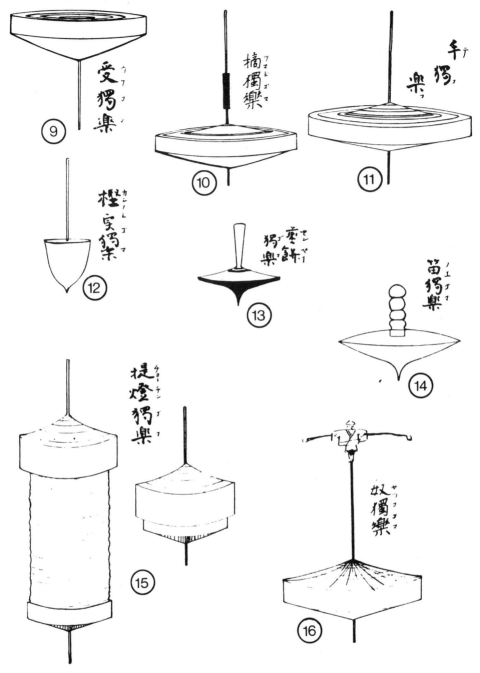

9. *Uke-goma,* catching-top.
10. *Tsumami-goma,* pinching-top.
11. *Te-goma,* hand-top.
12. *Kashinomi-goma,* acorn-top.
13. *Senpei-goma,* cake-top.
14. *Fue-goma,* whistle-top.
15. *Chochin-goma,* lantern-top.
16. *Yakko-goma,* slave-top.

Figure 106. Japanese tops, late nineteenth century; Group 2 (based on Culin).

terms are applied historically, which names are synthetic or derived from fanciful resemblance to other shapes, and which names may be applied only locally. Federli's linguistic studies show the need for caution in applying names to some European varieties of tops.

It is my general observation that twirlers (spun with the thumb and fingers) and many of the supported-tops from Japan are superior to European equivalents. Some of them have an extremely slender stem which predicates strong, tough material whose equivalent was not available to the European toymaker until the arrival of modern metallurgy. The union of the stem and body to attain balance bespeaks a high degree of mechanical skill. The reader's attention is directed to Figure 106, item 10, where the support or bracket is shown as a short piece of hollow reed slipped upon the top's stem. This device is easy to manipulate and, being inconspicuous, enhances the apparent skill of the spinner in placing the top in motion. Figure 107(c) also serves the purpose of a bracket.

Throughout Japanese descriptions of tops, mention is made of the iron-clad top, the *tetsudo*. The appellation brings to mind the peg-top of European notoriety often used in top "fighting" —the deliberate assault on the opponent's top with intent to inflict harm on it. But the *tetsudo* has no such use. Two notable features are that the metal peg is stout, but rounded instead of pointed, and that the circular rim of iron gives a weight distribution extremely favorable to momentum (Figure 108). In this *tetsudo* examined by us * the iron ring was three times the weight of the wooden body (approximately 110 grams vs. 37 grams). The distribution of much weight near the periphery allows a great deal of energy to be stored in the rotating top; the metal band is, in effect, a flywheel. It is estimated that this top when spun at a given speed will have five times the energy of rotation as a wholly wooden top of the same size spun at the same speed. This means that the heavier top, although encountering the same frictional resistance (air and peg) as the

* Courtesy of the late Dr. H. Waisman, Madison, Wis.

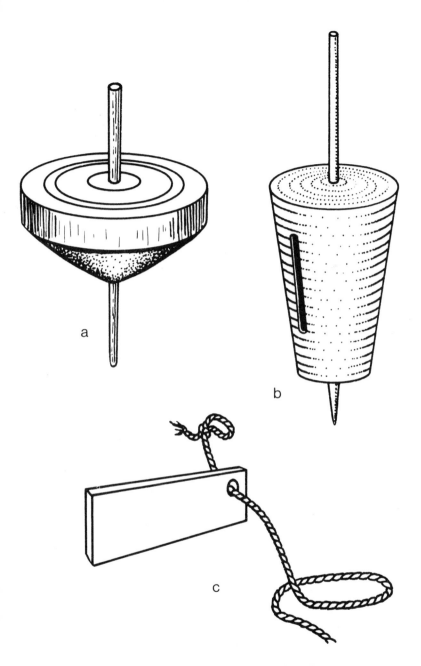

Figure 107 (a-h). Some representative Japanese tops (courtesy of H. Kano, 1969). (a) *Hakata;* (b) *Unari,* humming or groaning; (c) bracket and cord that can be used on all the tops except the *Muchi* and the *Suribachi.*

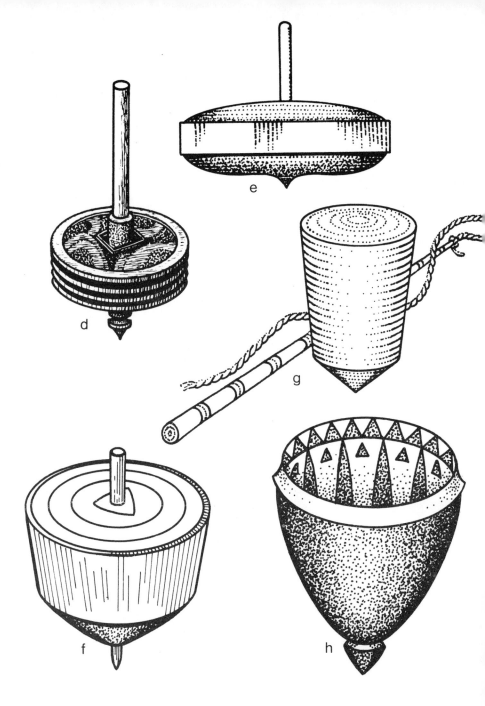

(d) *Zeni;* (e) *Hira;* (f) *Muchi;* (g) *Tetsudo;* (h) *Suribachi,*
hollow top of mortar from Hirosaki district.

lighter top, loses a proportionate amount of its energy (and speed) at a lesser rate. The top should spin longer and be less affected by a rough spinning surface. As far as we know, this concept of greatly augmented weight distribution is peculiar to the Orient. We spun this top with a makeshift bracket and probably fell short of the performance to be expected of its original owner. The toy is also operable as a peg-top.

Culin suggests the name *koma* means "solitary amusement" (see Figure 105, item 1). Since this is a supported-top and presumably a humming-top, the distinction seems to be made

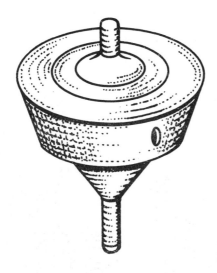

Figure 108. Tetsudo, or iron-clad, top. (Loaned by the late Dr. H. Waisman, 1969).

Figure 109. (a) "My top is better than your top," a supported top (courtesy of Mrs. K. S. MacIver); (b) the game of bai goma using peg-tops (based on Yamada).

from a group-play top such as the *bai goma* (Figure 105, item 2, and Figure 109b). Group play with peg-tops cast on a yielding surface such as a mat or rug spread over a tub has been discussed in the section Games Played With Tops.

Yamada shows illustrations of yo-yos, and Kano notes that this type of top was made of clay (ceramic?). (Figure 109a) shares the sentiment of Figures 76-77. Much original research on Oriental tops remains to be done in the libraries of China and Japan.

BIBLIOGRAPHICAL REFERENCES

Spring tops:	58, 61, 128
Disc:	15, 37
Exotic tops:	24, 41, 75, 76, 95, 203
Diavolo:	22, 28, 37, 41, 42, 55, 66, 81, 84, 88, 109, 125, 131, 189, 200, 204, 207, 208, 224, 245, 281, 347, 351
Plate and wand:	109
Silhouette:	347
Asian tops:	88, 212, 264, 303, 316, 361

La Promenade.

TECHNICAL ASPECTS

WHY THE TOP STANDS UP

WHEREAS THE bumblebee has been disparaged as an aerodynamic miscreation not logically expected to attain flight, many
mathematicians and physicists have rallied to the top's defense.
They have proved in abstruse terms that a spinning top should
assume an upright position and, accommodatingly, the top does
stand. This writer does not have the knowledge to choose between the merits of several analyses of the top's motion.*

Because the present author has failed to find satisfying ex-
planations of the spinning top's characteristic property—the
ability to stand upright—he has attempted to give a reasonable
explanation without stressing mathematics. This approach depends upon several precepts of high-school physics: Newton's

---

* In the bibliography, items of a mathematical nature are indicated as such,
if not apparent from the title.

First Law of Motion; possible motions of the wheel or top; rule of rotation and handgrasp; the parallelogram of forces; and precession.

Newton's First Law of Motion. We shall be concerned only with that part of Newton's Law that says that moving objects continue to move in a given direction unless acted upon by some other force. We may term this inertia. The condition of continued direction seems absurdly self-evident; it is the departure from the initial direction that alerts us that an outside force is being exerted. For example, if we take a hoop or wheel and roll it vigorously in an upright position on a level surface, it will move in a straight line. The plane of the hoop will be maintained perpendicular to the ground until the speed of the hoop is much diminished; the hoop may then wobble or run in a curved path. The loss of speed is due to air resistance and to contact of the wheel with irregularities of the ground.

Possible Motions of a Spinning Wheel (or Top). A rapidly rotating wheel resembles a spinning top. When any outside force acts upon a revolving wheel in a manner to disturb the alignment of the wheel's plane (or the wheel's axle) this force is resisted by the wheel's inertia. See Figure 110(a) where the wheel is assumed to be rotating with its axle OA. The axle is shown suspended from C, but it could be supported from below on a pivot at O; further, if the wheel is weightless, as an object would be in outer space, no support or suspension is needed. There are three motions the wheel may have: rotation on its axle OA (presumed throughout this section), pivoting so that the axle OA moves in a horizontal plane around point O and rotates the suspending axis CO; pivoting so that the axle OA tends to make an end-over-end movement in a vertical plane, turning the imaginary axis DOE.

Rule of Rotation and Handgrasp. The effect of the wheel in Figure 110(a) rotating on its principal axis OA may be represented at any instant by a line provided with an arrow (Figure 110b). The direction of the arrow is obtained as follows:

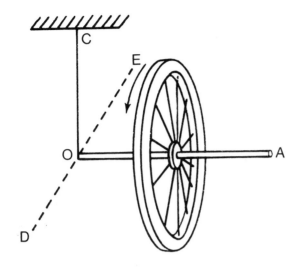

Figure 110a. Possible motions of a spinning wheel or a top.

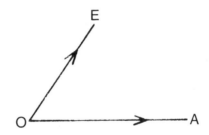

Figure 110b. Direction of forces in a spinning wheel.

Imagine that the four fingers of the right hand are put upon the upper surface of the axle OA and grasp it so that the fingers follow the revolving of the axle. Extend the thumb at right angles to the fingers, and the thumb will indicate the direction of the arrow. In Figure 110(b), the arrow will point toward A and away from O. If a downward force, for example, is applied at point A of Figure 110(a) so as to make the wheel and its axle pivot at O, this force is to be thought of as causing the imaginary axis DOE to turn slightly. The reader must bear in mind that the axes CO, DOE, and OA though shown as being away from the wheel, are so shown only for convenience; a vertical axis through the wheel's center, and a horizontal axis parallel to DOE could be drawn through a diameter of the wheel. Now in the present case where the wheel is tipped downward by a force at A, it is as though DOE is rotated slightly. Using the right-hand rule,* this axis at the particular instant of position will have an arrow pointing toward E. If the axle OA had been tilted up at A causing the axis DOE to rotate, the arrow of DOE would point to D. If the axle OA had been pivoted to move in a clockwise direction, the arrow of axis OC would point down. If the axle OA is pivoted horizontally about O in a counterclockwise direction, the arrow of OC would point toward C.

The Parallelogram of Forces. It is an established principle of physics that if two forces act upon a body at the same time, the condition and result can be expressed as a geometrical figure. In the Figure 111(a), the forces X and Y pull upon a body Z. The lengths of the lines ZX and ZY are proportional to the magnitude of the forces. (In our case it is not necessary to consider the length of the lines, only their direction.) Draw a parallelogram with opposite sides equal to ZX and ZY; draw the diagonal ZR. The direction of this diagonal obviously is a compromise in the directions of ZX and ZY (Figure 111b).

Refer again to Figure 110; the force represented by the wheel rotating on its axle OA has a direction toward A. The weight of the wheel moves the wheel and axle downward so that the pivoting at O gives a rotation to the axis DOE. This rotation will point the arrow of DOE toward E. The parallelogram of OA and OE with their respective arrows gives a resultant diagonal OR which may be thought of as lying somewhere in the

---

* A comparable rule could be set up using the left hand.

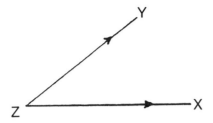

Figure 111a. Representation of two forces acting on a body.

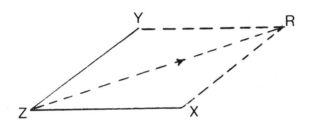

Figure 111b. Parallelogram of forces.

area EOA. This means that the wheel and its axle OA will try to pivot and move counterclockwise in a horizontal plane toward E.

Precession. The above combination of two forces such as the spinning of the wheel on its axle and rotating of the axis OC or DOE gives a resultant movement which is called precession. If the speed of rotation of the wheel on its axle is high enough and if the wheel's weight is not too great, the suspended system shown will rotate on the axis OC, apparently defying gravity. Instead of sinking down, the wheel and its axle move horizontally about O in a counterclockwise direction, and will continue to do so until friction greatly lessens the speed of the wheel's rotation on its axle.

Let us consider the wheel and its axle of Figure 110(a) as a spinning top with the axle standing almost vertically on a table-top (see Figure 111 a ; assume O is a peg). The wheel does not seem quite balanced, and at the moment may be leaning to the right. We know that the axle is trying to rotate the imaginary axis DOE and, from the handgrasp rule, the arrow of DOE points toward E. The combination of the forces OA and OE is to the left of OA, and the upper end of the axle OA moves to the left though the axle still leans outward. Point A describes a circle and the axle OA describes a cone. Eventually the top slows down, the axle OA leans out more and more, and the wheel is unable to keep from tipping over.

Now consider Figure 112(b) where the peg-point is exaggerated. The top is spinning counterclockwise and the peg is rubbing against the tabletop at F. (Actually there will be an area of rubbing, but we can regard the effect as being concentrated at a point.) The friction may be thought of as a force against the peg and in the direction toward the observer. While friction pushes against the peg, the body of the top receives no push and is free to move in a direction away from the observer. The top, as it is shown leaning outward to the right, is affected by gravity exerting a downward pull on the axle OA and this exerts a turning effort on the axis XFP. Using the handgrasp rule, we can give a directional arrow of XFP toward P, and OA toward A. The compromise of directions is between P and A so that the axle of OA tends to move to the left, i.e., seeks to assume a vertical position.

If the top's speed is high enough, the top soon reaches an upright stance, and perhaps spins with almost imperceptible motion. It is said to be "asleep." Then, as the top gradually slows down, any slight imbalance may cause the top to lean toward the side which is slightly heavier. The top precesses and the precession becomes wilder as it attempts to compensate for the slowing rotation. Finally the top falls over upon its side and rolls to a stop. In its last stages, the precession will often be seen as a series of loops described by the peg, while the upper part of the top makes a series of loops in the air.

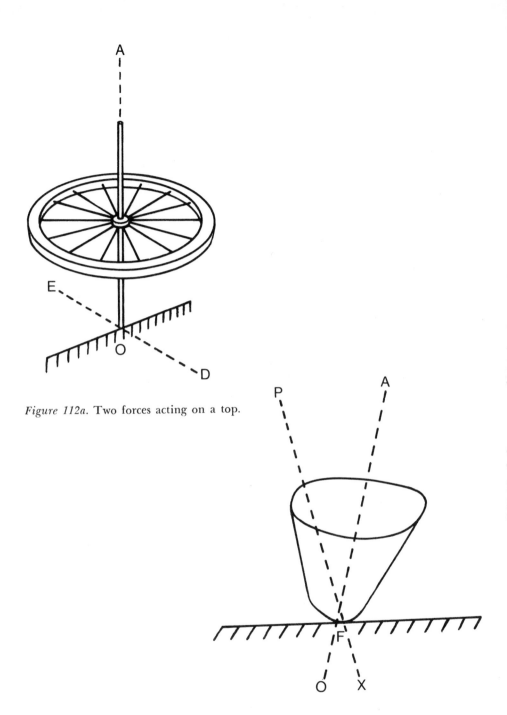

Figure 112a. Two forces acting on a top.

Figure 112b. Friction of peg causes the top to rise.

It is a curious phenomenon—friction of the top's peg against the table has brought the spinning top to a halt, but without friction of the peg on the table, the rotating top could not have come to an upright position. Only by chance could a peg-top be cast to land upright on a perfectly smooth table and remain upright. It is easier to make a peg-top with a short, blunt peg stand up than a top with a longer, slenderer peg, in part by reason of the difference in friction of the two pegs against the table surface.

HOW TO MAKE AN EGG BEHAVE AS A TOP

A Diplomatic Interlude; Second-Guessing a Navigator. Samuel Eliot Morison recounts the following story about Christopher Columbus:

> *Columbus being at a party with many noble Spaniards, where, as was customary, the subject of conversation was the Indies; one of them undertook to say:—"Señor Cristobal, even if you had not undertaken this great enterprise, we should not have lacked a man who would have made the same discovery as you did, here in our own country of Spain, as it is full of great men clever in cosmography and literature." Columbus made no reply, but took an egg and had it placed on the table saying: "Gentlemen, you make it stand there, not with crumbs, salt, etc. (for everyone knows how to do it with meal or sand) but naked and without anything at all, as I will, who was the first one to discover the Indies." They all tried, and no one succeeded in making it stand up. When the egg came round to the hands of Columbus, by beating it down on the table he fixed it, having thus crushed a little of one end; wherefore all remained confused, understanding what he meant; after the deed is done, everybody knows how to do it; and they ought first to have sought for the Indies, and not laugh at him who had sought for them first.*

It occurred to us that two alternatives to Columbus's egg-tapping episode might work. Suppose the egg were supported in a vertical position, with the large end down, in boiling water until hard-boiled, There is some likelihood of this object behaving like a top when spun, and of assuming an upright position on the smaller end. The raw egg is incapable of being a good top because the fluid contents give rise to an unstable center of rotation.* The other possibility would be to immerse the egg in dilute acid (say, vinegar) to soften the shell; the shell might then deform without breaking, and the egg would be able to stand on end. The first method was only modestly successful in making a hard-boiled egg spin (for further on the egg as a top, see Bouasse and Crabtree). With the second, it took about twenty-four hours for the vingear to render the shell soft enough so the egg would stand on end.

ROTATING SPEED OF A TOP

Until the stroboscope came into being, the world was divided into two camps as regards how fast a top spins. The first and somewhat larger group didn't care; the second group cheerfully settled upon a high figure. What is the stroboscope? The name derives from the Greek word *scopos*, to see, and happily, *strobos*, to turn or spin. The instrument, in effect, illuminates with a pulsating light the object whose speed is to be measured. If the number of pulses per unit time is the same as the number of revolutions in the same time, the spinning object seems to stand still.

Now stroboscopes aren't easy to come by; they are high-priced instruments, and their custodians need to be persuaded that the speed of a top is of any consequence.† The top-spinner must

---

* Much earlier Gray, too, noted that Columbus could have used a hard-boiled egg as a top.

† Acknowledging loan of Pioneer Electric Model 12 stroboscope by Atlantic-Richfield Co., Philadelphia.

meet terms as to where, when, and for how long the instrument will be used; he is nervous before a critical audience. No wonder; the best behaved tops can have erratic moments and failure to spin often occurs. Then there is the matter of causing the spinning object to perform in the field of the strobe, that is, the instrument must be focused upon some part of the top's surface. With a twirler, this is not too difficult; the constrained top, too, does quite well; but the peg-top, the yo-yo, and the diavolo can be exasperating. No attempt was made to measure the whip-top's speed.

The finely balanced wheels of today's gyroscope or the equivalent of Serson's top present no problem; the rate of decay of speed after the initial impulse is low, and the strobe can be brought to focus quickly. The common top, however, loses speed from bearing-point friction and from air resistance. The researcher will be content with the expression "at least . . . rpm."

Shown below is a sampling of results with a few specimens of tops.

Twirler. Plastic, 1¼″ diameter, weight 1.81 grams, general shape that of Figure 86; spins very steadily for 20 or more seconds. Rotating speeds 3,200–3,400 rpm.

Supported-top. Wood, with metal axis; 2⅛″ diameter, shape approximately that of Figure 104, item 27. Speed 2,200 rpm.

Buzzer. Plastic button, 1⅜″ diameter, length of cord (doubled) 24″; weight 8.81 grams. Speed 3,000–4,000 rpm.

Spring-top. Metal, like Figure 88. Speed 2,000–3,200 rpm.

Diavolo. Plastic cones, 4″ diameter by 2¾″ height. Speed 1,800 rpm.

Yo-yo. Plastic shells, 2¼″ diameter; like Figure 57; weight 17.04 grams. Speed 1,200 rpm at low point of drop. A heavier top (weight 45.07 grams) recorded 1,800 rpm.

Peg-top. Speed 3,400 rpm.

What conclusions may be drawn as to the significance of these tests? Very few, although we think the tests are duplicable with the same equipment. The high speed of the buzzer is remarkable, but in retrospect it seems that the speeds that this author attained were much lower than if persons adept with a particular type of top did the spinning. This, however, we leave to other researchers.

THE SPIN OF A BALL IN SPORT

If the reader will take an object readily held in the hand, grasping it with the thumb and fingers, and will throw the object (not toss or lob it) the object rolls from the fingers and acquires a rotary motion as well as a forward one. The rotation is clockwise for a right-handed person. In the game of baseball, the pitcher throws the ball in a manner to enhance the spin naturally imparted. In its flight (about 60½ feet between pitcher and batter) the ball is said to rotate at about 1,800 rpm and move toward the batter at a speed of 70 miles or more per hour. The ball creates air turbulence and moves perceptibly from a simple parabolic path, thus adding to the problems of the batter who attempts to judge the time and position of the ball upon its arrival. It will be understood that the pitcher can in some measure cause the ball to curve away from the normal line of flight. The table below shows conditions.

SPEED OF PITCHED BALL		TIME OF FLIGHT	DISTANCE BALL WILL DROP DUE TO GRAVITY
Miles/hour	*Feet/second*	*Seconds*	*Feet*
50	73	.83	8.6
70	102	.60	5.8
75	110	.56	5.0
80	117	.53	4.4
85	124	.50	3.9
90	132	.47	3.5

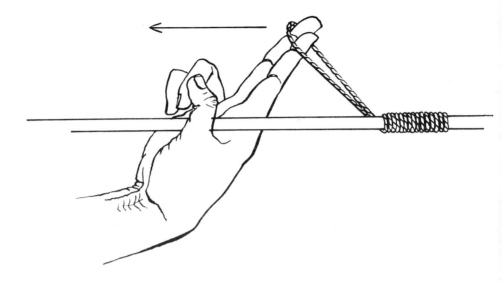

Figure 113. Manner of casting the Olympic Games javelin in classical Greek times. Accuracy rather than distance was sought (based on Gardiner).

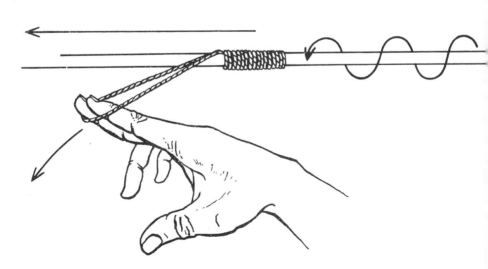

The effort of giving controlled spin (and curvature of flight) is said to be extremely tiring to the pitcher.

In tennis, the cut given by the racket to the ball is an example of augmenting spin in relation to forward motion. Golf, too, furnishes examples. Ordinarily, the drive is an almost square impact of the club-head upon the ball, giving it only moderate spin. The variants where the impact is not square are known as hook, slice, bite, and overspin.

Curiously, the ability of rotation to impart control in flight seems to have been known to the athletes of the Olympic Games during classical Greek times. Gardiner shows (Figure 113) how the javelin thrower took advantage of this where accuracy in casting, rather than distance, was sought. If Gardiner's representation is valid, it will be apparent that rapid rotation of the shaft was possible, and the motion of the javelin was the equivalent of that found in a cast peg-top.

HUMAN BEINGS AS TOPS

The figures of speech like "a whirling Dervish" or "spun like a teetotum" occur with moderate frequency in literature, likening the persons involved to spinning tops. The expressions have aptness. There is a Moslem sect, the Mevlani or Maulavi, whose rites have been sustained since the thirteenth century. These rites include dancing with very exacting demands made upon aspiring novices. Witnesses of the dancing have marked the unison and great physical effort attained; despite the sect's repute as "whirling Dervishes" they are essentially a meditative order. The extraordinary dance, performed to simple rhythmic music, requires the group of performers to whirl about the hall individually. The whirl is intensive and is made upon the left foot, the right foot serving as the pusher. The rate of rotation has been noted at forty-five turns a minute and may continue for forty minutes or more. The vigor of the action is well attested by observers; Figure 114 is said to be a good likeness of

Figure 114. Dervish of the Mevlani or Maulavi sect (based on Lane).

a performer. There is no ill effect to the dancers, and despite the ecstasy of the performers, they seem to have complete control in response to their leader's directions. The balancing of the dervish in an upright position and of the pirouetting skater alike depend upon the forces manifested in the spinning top.

The comparison to a teetotum is a favorite way of describing the unlucky human target who comes within the gunsights of the hero in many good Western movies. But Boas, cited by Culin [90] describes the following peculiar to the Eskimo:

> *A large cake of ice is formed in the shape of a top with a flat surface above and a dull point below which fits into a shallow hole in the ice-pack. Generally a man who is the butt of all the others is induced to sit on this top, and is spun around until he is made sick.*

Time was (and yet may be) when a whirling platform was offered fun seekers at amusement parks in this century. Here, we can say the subject acted of his free will. The platform was what one might call a human centrifuge. It consisted of a circular disc twelve to twenty feet in diameter, with a smooth hardwood finish and set flush with the floor. Equipped with a mechanical drive and controlled by the will of a sadistic operator, it offered a huge challenge to withstand centrifugal forces. With the machine at rest, the fun seekers swarmed onto the disc, the more agile and aggressive sought the center; the timid, cautious, and belated individuals perforce occupied the outer areas.

As the disc was accelerated, voices were stilled; grim, even haggard expressions were shown. At this stage, any ejection seldom involved just one individual, because any person occupying an inner position who had his hold loosened inevitably carried with him anyone in his path. Finally there might remain one player, the one who had the choice position at the center of the disc. He strove to maintain a nice distribution of his anatomy on either side of the axis of rotation. And now began a grim duel between operator and player. A slight imbalance is felt, the palms become moist, the slip starts and, with a swoosh, the player is hurled outward. Note, however, that though his angular speed is not much greater than where other players were ejected, he must pass through the entire radius, and as he finally encounters maximum peripheral speed he resembles a missile catapulted into the spectators.

A variant of this amusement was to run counter-rotationally on the disc. This involved an awareness and avoidance of bodies. Miscalculation might result in heavy falls and mutual recriminations. Such are the sad pleasures (but it was fun) of two cultures (Eskimo and American) separated by a mere 30° of latitude.

THE TOP AS WEAPON

Apart from the drastic forms of top-play (previously discussed under the peg-top) especially the so-called split-peg top, whose use carried the *intent* to inflict harm, children's play with tops has remained play.

However, it is said that a yo-yo type of top has been used by certain Filipino tribes as a weapon. The aggressor takes a position in a tree beside a trail where his enemy is expected to pass, and at the suitable moment, the heavy yo-yo is thrown to strike the intended victim on the head. Presumably the top's owner would be skillful enough to administer a second blow, if needed, because of quick recovery of the top. We lack direct evidence to the contrary, and can only express mild skepticism. The yo-yo depends upon its rotary motion and inertia to rewind upon the cord. This would preclude full striking force such as possessed by a free missile. The top would have to be hurled with a very nice calculation of the distance from thrower to victim. Any number of conditions can be visualized whereby the top, after striking, would not rewind properly.

Of unknown antiquity is the use of a projectile whose shape and motion bear resemblance to the Frisbee as a weapon. Among the Sikhs of India, it seemingly was associated with the *Chakra*, discus of the god Vishnu, which resembles a wheel or quoit (Figure 89b).It is made of steel, six to nine inches in diameter, with the outer edge ground very sharp. It was whirled about on the forefinger and might be projected fifty to eighty yards. Greater distance has been claimed, but unless correlation with weight and size is made, such claims have less importance. Yet there has been cited the casting of a disc weighing over half a pound to a distance of 530 feet with a fall in vertical distance of about 6 feet, an astonishing aerodynamic performance. Despite the fact that the missile is almost useless as a weapon because of man's inability to attain good accuracy in throwing, it may be guessed it might have been an effective weapon at short range in pre-firearms days when cast by a skilled Sikh warrior.

Bogaert, in his very broad treatment of gyroscopic effects, shows that the flight of the boomerang is related to the gyro. The boomerang is known both as toy and as a weapon; it is usually associated with adult use. Kaudern's observation [221] on sling-stones resembling tops has been cited. Modern warfare leans heavily on the gyro for guidance of man and missile.

THE TOP AS AN EARLY AID TO NAVIGATION

The Gropings of an Illiterate Mechanic into Navigation.

Geometers can prove and ship captains have trusted that if the date and time of day are known, one can measure the height of the sun above the horizon, and thereby determine the latitude (distance north or south of the equator) at which the observation is made. The more precise the time and angular measurement, the more certain the location. Although the horizon at sea has the advantage of not being cluttered by trees and houses, this advantage diminishes or vanishes if haze is present. The sun may be shining brilliantly, but any measurement is cast in doubt by uncertainty as to where the line of sea and sky meet. And the difficulty is compounded because even in a quiet sea, there is a gentle pitch or roll to the ship.

No studied development of navigational aids will be made here; it is enough to follow through the original thinking of a keen observer of an important property of tops, the ability to assume an upright position when spinning. John * Serson reasoned in this fashion: if the body of a top is given a flat upper surface at right angles to the major axis of the top, then this surface will be horizontal when the top is spinning. If the surface is mirrored or polished, it becomes a useful artificial horizon regardless of haze. Serson appears to have been a very competent mechanic and his device was tested by and for the British Admiralty in 1743. On land or upon inland waters, the results were gratifying; in coastal waters, the top was affected by the motion of the ship (an Admiralty yacht). Refinements were made to the instrument, and it was installed and sent to sea in HMS *Victory* in 1744. The ship was wrecked; all hands and the inventor were lost; and we can never know how well or badly the instrument performed.

In 1752, John Smeaton tested a model of Serson's design, spinning it in air and in a vacuum. He noted that the top maintained "perfect horizontality" for fifteen minutes and spun for two hours in a vacuum. Figure 115 shows the essentials of the invention; the actual machine is a tribute to the instrument-maker's art. The Admiralty, however, dropped interest in the matter; others who tried the device found it "imperfect," requiring the attention of a skilled operator. And so passed from

---

* Thanks to the National Maritime Museum, Greenwich, England; most accounts of the inventor and his work do not dignify Serson with a given name.

▶

Figure 115. Principal features of Serson's navigational top; (a) is a heavy disc, mirrored on its upper surface. When rotated at high speed, the disc takes and maintains a horizontal stance. The line of sight S-a to eye gives the angular height of the sun above the real and artificial horizon. (Based on *Gentlemen's Magazine,* October 1754).

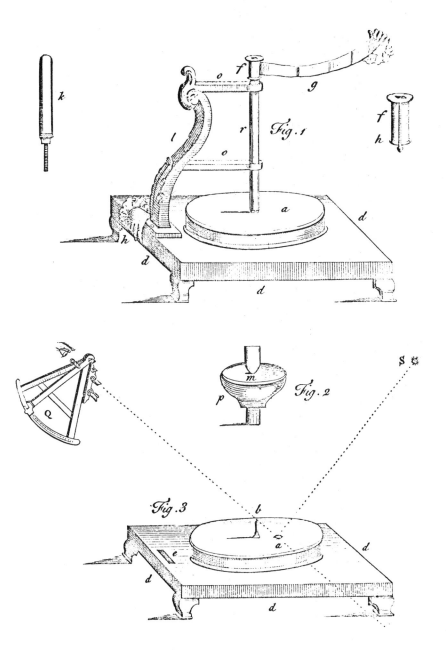

Fig. 1

Fig. 2

Fig. 3

practical navigation the use of the invention. To Serson for his originality of thought and the respectability he sought to give the top, we gratefully restore to him the name, John.

In the early 1800s, Edward Troughton of Northumberland, England, further improved Serson's top, but it never gained Admiralty acceptance. It was estimated that the peripheral speed of the rotor was 30 miles per hour, probably equivalent to a rotational speed of 2,000 rpm. Again it should be noted that these early experimenters were aware of the drag of the air upon the top, and they obtained remarkable duration of spinning in a partial vacuum. To Troughton (1753–1835) we owe two distinct debts for his association with tops; he kept alive the memory of John Serson and he attempted to gauge the top's speed. The very act of seeking a quantitative measurement was a sure sign that the new Industrial Age was coming into being.

An officer in the French Marine, Georges-Ernest Fleuriais (1840–1895) with more influence on the authorities than Serson could ever have had, conducted a long series of trials with a modified model of the top. Again, there was less than total satisfaction with the results, but the device spurred efforts with alternate means—improved sextants.

The ripple caused by the ill-starred Serson had a far-reaching succession of events, culminating in reliable instruments for air navigation as well as marine. There was a curious fusion of the astronomers' wish to explain the motion of the Earth with the mariners' need to explain the apparent position of the heavenly bodies in relation to the position of the observer on this planet. The elements of the device we call a gyroscope were emerging.

THE GYROSCOPE

The movement of Earth through space has been likened to that of a top, and astronomers have attempted mechanical models. The German, Johann Gottlieb Bohnenberger, devised a model that contributed greatly to the clarity of discussions.

Jean Bernard Leon Foucault (1819–1868) built upon the accomplishments of his predecessors and contemporaries and, with interests divided between physics and astronomy, showed his own device, which he called a gyroscope, to explain the behavior of celestial bodies. There then followed an incident that carried a remarkable and practical social lesson.

The Royal Society (London) in 1850 bestowed on Foucault the prized Copley Medal for his demonstration of the gyroscope. The announcement of the award called forth a protest from Edward Sang who declared that in 1836, he had delivered a talk in which the principles of the gyroscope were described. Sang's talk was thereupon printed, but never overcame the headway of Foucault in the public mind. In justice to both men, we can look upon the matter as a coincidence. Piracy of ideas need not be imputed to Foucault; his occupation as an astronomer and experimental physicist would likely keep him informed of technical developments throughout Europe, and there is no evidence that Sang insisted his ideas should be kept secret. It is certain that Foucault had a gyroscope model made and that he expounded lucidly upon the implications of the gyroscopic principles in the movement of Earth. To Foucault may justly be credited awareness, and from this has stemmed a formidable succession of technical applications. Sang tacitly owned to being at some fault by saying that the press of other matters had intervened to delay continued development work on his ideas.

A modest review of scientific effort in the nineteenth century convinces one that a massive attack on the behavior of the top was in progress. Bohnenberger in Germany, Foucault in France,* Sang in Britain, and Johnson in America produced apparatus that differed very little in design and were used to interpret the problems confronting the researcher. It is almost a truism that

---

* France recently honored Foucault by depicting this scientist on a postage stamp (Scott No. 871) shown in Figure 116. The United States has given similar distinction to such scientists as Benjamin Franklin and Alexander Graham Bell.

JEUX D'ENFANTS

II. La Toupie
Impromptu

Transcription pour Piano à 2 mains
par Lucien GARBAN

Georges BIZET
Op. 22

Figure 116a. The top's sound set to music by Bizet.

Figure 116b. French stamp of Foucault, inventor of the gyroscope.

if Foucault had not designed (and applied, explained, and published) the gyroscope, the equivalent would have been available in a short time. The genius of a generation following these four innovators has lifted the status of the gyroscope from that of a scientific top to that of an indispensable adjunct to applied technology.

The application of the gyroscope as a stabilizer and as a navigational aid are largely twentieth-century accomplishments. As a navigational aid, it is the heart of many instruments, and in fact it may be said that until the advent of electronics, it was the principal device. For example, the gyro can be coupled to a compass so that a ship's course, once determined, may be held automatically without human intervention, regardless of wind, currents, or the local magnetic north. The gyroscope's darker face appears when its principles are applied to the guidance of the torpedo and ballistic missile.

In the gyroscope we have a remarkable toy.* The mechanism most probably familiar to us is the wheel revolving in a cage (Figure 117). The exterior poles of this cage are usually provided with a dimple on one end and a groove on the other. These enable the top to perform spectacular feats of standing on a point or upon an edge.

As with the mathematics of the top as a whole, the behavior of the gyroscope will be left to the highly competent. Fortunately the literature is adequate, and some citations will be found in any sizable library. Herewith are two we think very good: Bouasse presents many variants of the gyroscope as a laboratory tool, giving no references, but providing an excellent text (in French) and illustrations; Crabtree and Perry give lucid descriptions without emphasis on mathematics.

---

* It is astonishing how rapidly Foucault's term gyroscope spread. U.S. Patent 24430 issued June 14, 1859, to Francis Milward reads, in part, ". . . a philosophical toy, designed to illustrate . . . motions and forces incident to gyroscopes and spinning tops."

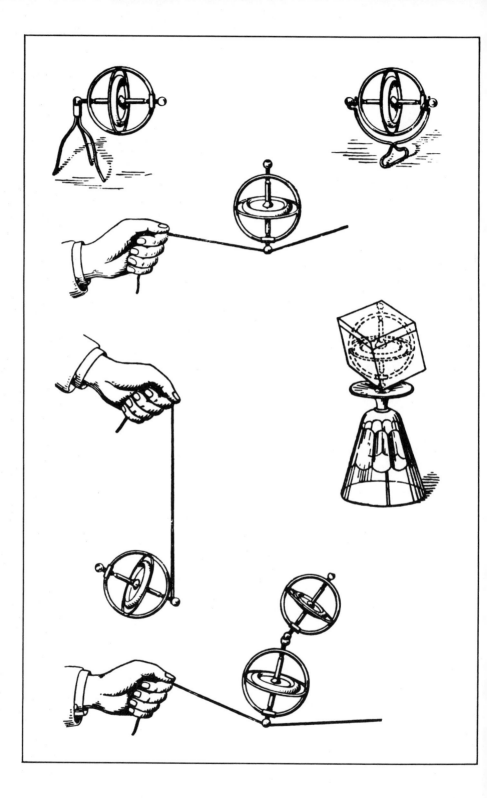

EARTH AS A TOP

Gray (among others) compared the gyroscope to a top, then said the earth is a gyroscope and thus, the earth is a top. Very early definitions of the top included the concept that it was a body with rotary motion; there also may be translatory motion. Our planet rotates with a peripheral speed at the equator of about 1,000 miles an hour or ⅓ mile a second. Some tentative efforts we made to estimate a peg-top's speed with a stroboscope yielded a figure about one-fiftieth that of the earth. Now the earth in its orbit about the sun speeds along at 20 miles a second. In this flight, the earth would seem to resemble a projectile hurtling through space. But the analogy must end; the projectile as fired from a rifled gun spins about its major axis. Our perverse planet may spin almost broadside to its line of flight, a matter of little consequence as there is no resisting medium for the spin to act upon.

BIBLIOGRAPHICAL REFERENCES

Why the top stands up:	20, 41, 75, 84, 159, 161
How to make an egg stand up (and behave like a top):	161, 258
Spin of an object in sport:	34, 140, 144
Human beings as tops:	47, 90, 185, 234, 261, 345
The top as weapon:	15, 221
Aid to navigation:	304, 309
The gyroscope:	16, 17, 37, 41, 75, 84, 98, 129, 130, 161, 162, 215, 269, 272, 304

◄

Figure 117. Some aspects of the toy gyroscope (based on Crabtree).

· CHAPTER EIGHT ·

OF MATTERS SPIRITUAL AND PERSONAL

THE TOP has no spiritual significance in Christendom today. Throughout Europe and the Americas it is regarded simply as a juvenile toy, a seasonal fad perhaps. There are instances in the past when the top assumed a larger role, but one looks in vain for an explanation of its importance at the time and for its decline. Observe the intent expression of the person watching the top in Figure 21. Some scholars interpret this fragment of classical Greek art as the reading of destiny in the turn of Fortune's wheel. And the violent disruption of the top-spinning evidenced in Figure 5(e) seems to indicate intervention by a higher power. The discovery of top-like objects in archaeological sites seems to indicate that a votive offering and provision for amusement in afterlife were an integral part of classical beliefs. Ceramic tops such as shown in Figure 5(c,d) might be recovered from a sanctuary or as gravegoods; the archaeologists must guess at the relation of the toy to its onetime owner.

Early in the Christian Era, top-spinning by adults carried no disapprobation, although later it was deplored (by Basil) as a waste of time. There is a tantalizing bit of medieval information from approximately A.D. 800–1200 furnished by Hone: "According to a story (whether true or false) in one of the churches of Paris, a choir boy used to *whip a top* marked with *alleluia* written in gold letters, from one part of the choir to the other." The significance of the word and the action is elusive. One version says that the ceremonial "Burial of Alleluia" was sung in churches from Easter to Pentecost, and a turf or large piece of sod was borne in the manner of a coffin through the church to the parish place of interment. No convincing explanation has been found; perhaps the ritual interment represented final disposal of some of Man's shortcomings (thus equivalent to forgiveness and absolution). The whipping of the top might be another aspect of the biblical scapegoat, that is, placing of punishment upon a substitute culprit.

The reader who is in a mind to contemplate the writings of John Brady in his exposition upon church holy days will perhaps reach an opinion whether "whipping tops" was or was not approved by the clergy. I was baffled by Brady's intricacies and retained only the thought that top-spinning was once sanctioned by some church fathers. Brueghel's classic painting of children's games (Figure 118) includes young top-spinners whose garb and locale seem somewhat monastic. The youth in the left archway is whipping a top; to the right, a peg-top is being spun.

The stained glass window of a fifteenth-century church (Figure 119) shows further evidence of the permissiveness extended to tops. The scene is from the Savile Chapel, built about 1447 at the Thornhill parish church (Yorkshire). The subject of the window was the family of Zebedee (Matt. 4, 21); two children, James and John, are shown playing at whip-top.

Figure 118. Brueghel's "Games"; note top-spinners in porch (courtesy Kunsthistorischens Museum, Vienna).

Figure 119. Stained glass window (1466) in chapel at Thornhill, England. Portion shown is said to represent two boys
of the family of Zebedee playing at whip-top (based on
Dewsbury Guide).

No spiritual significance seems attached to the intrusion of the *dreidel* (top) in Hanukkah celebrations. The fast shrinking Stone Age culture of the Maoris does offer direct evidence of spiritual meaning ascribed to the mundane top. Songs were sung to the accompaniment of humming-tops. Words and melodies * have been recorded by anthropologists. Hamilton [181] says that the sound of the humming-top gave solace to the defeated warrior. In a culture where defeat in war was much more than a bruising of communal pride and carried with it almost certain harsh treatment, the top evidently afforded some spiritual escape from bitter reality.

PERSONAL ASPECTS

If this description of tops has reflected a personal admiration for the toy and the pastime, it is but to be expected that those of contrary opinion will have also voiced their low esteem of tops and top-spinners. We herewith cite instances, but attempt to gainsay the detractions:

Basil (later Saint Basil) gained fame for his sermons delivered to an audience drawn from the top-spinning set, that is, the idlers. To Basil, the inroads he could make upon their wasted hours was clear gain in eternity. (History doesn't record whether this era, about A.D. 365, was the twilight of Western adult top-spinning.)

There was the churlish dismissal of John Serson's speculum top (1744) as an aid to navigation. Some of his countrymen wrote: ". . . but it was cumbersome and required great skill in use. It soon disappeared." This sounds suspiciously as though some pious wish had been granted.

Sixteen pages of text from an article by Starr [319] with the very likely title "Japanese Toys and Toy-Collectors" states: ". . . kites, windmills, tops, whistles and the like. We but mention them."

---

* Recalling, for the music conscious, the little pianoforte piece composed by Georges Bizet in 1871 and shown in Figure 116.

Then again, a father, urging his son to go to school will say, "Go and learn, son"; but the son on his way to school meets companions who persuade him to play tops with them. The father reacts by saying to himself, "Tops have more immediate interest." The scene is neither Republican Rome nor Victorian England—it is Borneo.

The *Saturday Review* (London, 1884) was a respected sounding board for the scholar, and in two closely printed columns one scholar has embalmed the top in scholarly phrases and concludes ". . . tops can hardly claim the interest and peculiar nationality of marbles. It would be almost as interesting to know who invented the handle (support) of the humming top as to know the name Achilles bore when in petticoats." In reply to the quotation above, the invention of the handle was brilliant; the inventor's identity and Achilles' other name are alike lost.

Of North Australia, Torres Strait country, the following was said: "Top-spinning was very prevalent; indeed the people played at it so assiduously every weekday that they had no time to attend to their gardens, and on Saturday they did not bring in enough food to last until Monday. The Puritan Sunday in full force, none would dream of breaking it by gathering food, consequently numbers of children came to school Monday morning without having had breakfast. This made them peevish and inattentive, and an edict was issued prohibiting top matches on Saturdays, and the men were told to go to their gardens as before." It is probable the less tractable Malayans would have sent their women and children to the gardens (and continued the play).

Finally there is this poem:

Yes it's sweet to grouse about the crops,
And sweet to hear the tales the natives tell,
To watch the king and chieftains playing leisurely at tops,
While the country's bowling gaily down to hell.

HUGH CLIFFORD
(adapted from Rudyard Kipling)

One can hardly grudge the top-spinner a smirk of satisfaction; he and his sport have outlasted the critics; nor has his country yet sustained the threatened end.

BIBLIOGRAPHICAL REFERENCES

43, 45, 99, 105, 150, 151, 181, 201, 239, 299, 311, 319, 331, 334

WORD LIST

THE APPEARANCE of top-spinning terms, often without full explanation by authors, can be puzzling. The dictionary may not clear up the matter entirely. Listed below are some terms taken from material cited in the bibliography. In the case of conflicting definitions, reliance was placed on the context; the choice given here is arbitrary.

aerial top	a flying propeller
bandilor	the cast yo-yo (often walking)
bembix	whip-top of classical Greece
boxer	an English top presumably made of boxwood
bracket	a device to hold or constrain the top when starting. Synonyms are cage, handle, holder, key, standard, sprocket, yoke
bromtol	a humming-top

brumm topf	a humming-top
buxum	boxwood whip-top of the Romans
buzzer	a top also known as a whizzer, magic-wheel, or rhombus
chipstone	English game where objects such as stones were placed within a circle and peg-tops were cast to knock these stones from the circle
devil among the tailors	equivalent to a miniature game of skittles
devil on two sticks	the diavolo
diable	diavolo
domino	the die-top or teetotum
dreidel (dredl)	the Hanukkah teetotum (see *trendel*)
Dutch rackets	game played with a racket-shaped board having indentations to receive peg of spinning top and score for the player
émigrant (émigré, émigrette)	yo-yo
flying propeller	see index and Figure 19, item 44
gig	English whip-top
gillie-mirein	general term from Argyleshire for the top
gully	an English peg-top; also the game
gyrograph	a curve-tracing top
habergais	an Alsatian whip-top
hoaty	an English peg-top
hoges	English game played with whip-top
Kreisel (Keusel, Kusel, Krusel)	a German top
magic wheel	the classical buzzer, rhombus

Moench	a German term usually given to the peg-top from its fancied resemblance to a hooded monk
moyne	French term for whip-top
Nonne	German top resembling a nun
nonne	French term often given to the peg-top
pear	English peg-top, from shape of fruit
peeries	English peg-tops
peg-in-the-ring	an English game
peonza	general Spanish term for the top
piao	general Portuguese term for top
pinching-top	top set in motion by the action of a spring (tops shown in Figure 88 use this feature)
priktol	Dutch term for the peg-top
rotoscope	the gyroscope-like instrument of W. R. Johnson
sabot	French term for whip-top
Schnarchhaus	German term for humming-top
schnurrbas (schnurror, schnurrpreisel)	Scandinavian term for humming-top
slash	whip
spinner	general term for small top set in motion by finger action; teetotum
strobilos	Greek top
strombos	Greek top
teetotum shot	English game played with marbles and teetotum
tol (toppe, top, topsch)	general Dutch terms for top
toupie (toupe)	general French terms for top, especially the peg-top
traveling-top	the cast yo-yo

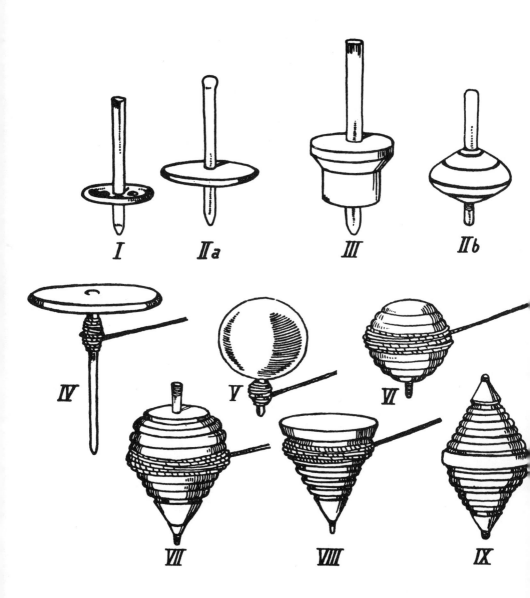

Figure 120. Top forms cited by Federli (based on Jaberg and Jud).

trendel (trendl)	Hanukkah teetotum
Triesel	another German term for *Kreisel*
trompe (trompo)	the whip-top
trottola	general Italian term for top
turbo	Latin for top
whizzer	buzzer
yo-yo	a general term for the confined top; also specifically used to mean the cast, recuperative top

The reader is particularly directed to Federli [120] whose exhaustive treatment of names of tops greatly exceeds the above word list. However, it must be noted that Federli was primarily interested in linguistics and his treatment of the top as an object is minor. Not shown by Federli, but serving as a guide to the top forms whose names he encountered, is Figure 120 (after Jud [219]). Items I, II, III are spun with the fingers, that is they are twirlers. Items IV and V are equivalents of the supported-top. Items VI, VII, VIII, IX could be used as peg-tops, but VIII and IX are expressly named as whip-tops. There is a fertile field for linguists in tracing the names of other top forms.

BIBLIOGRAPHICAL REFERENCES

110, 120, 257

REPRESENTATIVE
LITERATURE AS RELATED
TO GEOGRAPHICAL
LOCATION

Sometimes we find it convenient to approach a larger subject by seeking out what we know best of it. So with top-spinning, it is comforting to know that our area, our culture, our time is represented and has a tangible place in the whole. The presence of the top has been noted from Alaska to deep in South America, and circumferentially around the world. The remarkable resemblance of whip-tops from many widely separated localities is evidence either of diffusion of knowledge or repeated invention. Particularly notable are the remote and isolated Pacific island cultures. If' one accepts the diffusion theory, this connotes a very great lapse of time, beside which the specimens from classical antiquity must appear young indeed. If, on the other hand, independent invention is supposed to have given rise to the whip-top, it would seem that the opportunity to observe and modify the shape to afford good performance must have attended stable cultures with some respite from the demands of a hand-to-mouth existence.

In the following text we shall note the top in a number of

cultures. This is intended only as indicative, and the literature will reveal many examples. The listing not only is incomplete, it tends to overemphasize. If a single article on Malta is cited, this places it on near apparent parity with Japan about which a half dozen articles may be found. If a preponderance relates to the South Pacific areas, this is because of the large number of studies made upon primitive cultures and communities just beginning to feel the impact of the West. Scenes that long ago disappeared from Europe are no longer newsworthy, yet the immediate and present viability of top-spinning may be in as much danger of disappearing in Europe as is top-spinning in societies newly emerging from close contact with Stone Age cultures.

BIBLIOGRAPHICAL REFERENCES

AFRICA

Egypt	134, 277, 278, 279
French Equatorial Africa	25, 166, 338
Liberia	74

ASIA

Borneo	156, 299
Burma	179
Celebes	221
China	93, 134, 179, 224
India	11, 153, 168
Indonesia	206
Japan	13, 94, 167, 179, 207, 316, 347, 348, 361

A PATENTABLE
INVENTION

With even a cursory look at the literature of tops, one might suppose that all had been told of the ingenuity of man in discovering new forms of the toy. But no—since the inception of the United States Patent Office, inventors have been granted hundreds of documents which attest to the novelty claimed by the inventor. There is no intent to depreciate the patent offices of other countries, indeed, many United States patentees are of other nationality.

According to the classification system of the Patent Office, amusement devices and toys belong to the major class 46. Shown below is the subclass 47 which includes spinners and whirling devices.

CLASS 46   AMUSEMENT DEVICES, TOYS

47   SPINNING AND WHIRLING DEVICES

48   With sparking

49   With chromatic effects

50	Gyroscope
51	Whirlers
52	Sounding
53	Air actuated
55	Figure operating
56	Jet operated
57	Convection operated
58	Pinwheels
59	Self-winding spindle
60	Aerial tops
61	Tethered
62	Cord twist
63	Sounding
64	Tops
65	Combined
66	With sounding means
67	With spinning devices
68	Spiral
69	Spring impellers
70	Cord impellers
71	Holding means
72	Separable
73	Tips and spindles

Example: The gyroscopic top has classification of 46-50.

Shown in the table below is the number of patents issued (to 1967) in the subclasses 60 through 73:

SUBCLASS	NUMBER OF PATENTS
60	19
61	62
62	35

SUBCLASS	NUMBER OF PATENTS
63	64
64	56
65	60
66	58
67	69
68	27
69	63
70	44
71	25
72	65
73	29

There are other subclasses that actually involve features of the top, as, for instance, No. 50, Gyroscope. With all its faults, the system works, and if the reader has a better top than the world has hitherto known, his aim should be to secure a patent number and let the classification fall where it may. The number of U.S. patents is now well over three million.

From out of the several hundred patents relating to tops, a few are shown in Figure 121:

(a) 3233359, Class 46-61, a sound-producing top in which the elements of the yo-yo are recognizable.

(b) 2906057, Class 46-64, a top which when spun on its rounded body will invert to spin on the projecting shaft. This toy is a variant of Tippe Top.

(c) 3983498, Class 46-65, a curve-tracing top. See also "Barus [19]" in bibliography.

(d) 3263362, Class 46-67, rotatable top and spinner. Can this be related to a whip-top in which successive strokes renew the spinning energy?

(e) 2767514, Class 46-71; substitute a ball for the wheel and you have the equivalent of item 21, Figure 19.

(f) 2937472, Class 46-72, spinning top and holder. The peg no longer frustrates would-be spinners.

It would seem that the mobility of the population in the United States has tended to hold down the number of common names given to tops in contrast to some European areas. However, the Patent Office registry of trade marks exhibits plenty of names given to tops by manufacturers to promote sales. We are glad that tops have official recognition by national governments, and seldom have an ideological significance.*

* A notable exception is George Cruikshank's "The Corsican Whipping Top in Full Spin," which caricatures Napoleon's difficulties, 1814 (Figure 50).

Figure 121. Patents illustrating types of tops. (a) Tippe Top; (b) Yo-yo; (c) equivalent of Barus gyrograph, i.e., the peg point traces curves; (d) constrained, recuperative top; (e) the top is "whipped" by a revolving brush; (f) supported-top and bracket.

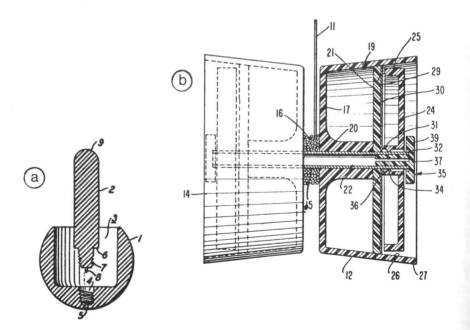

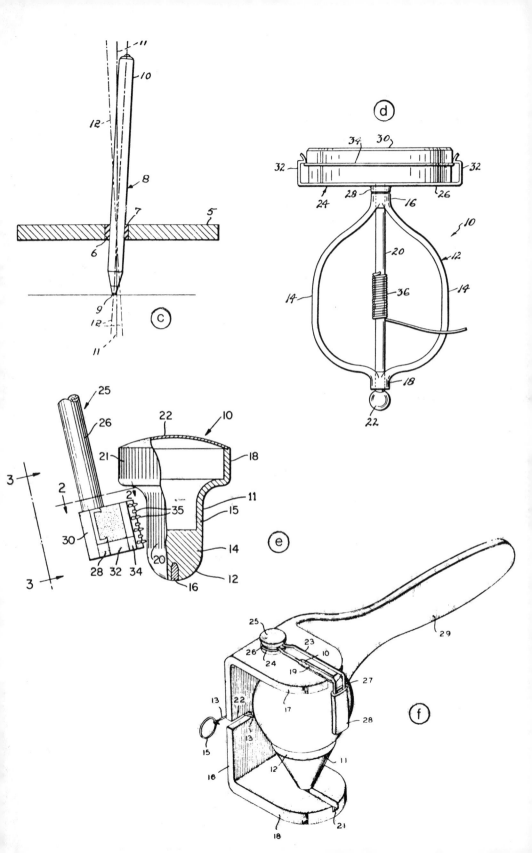

BIBLIOGRAPHY

THE AUTHOR has straddled the question confronting anyone compiling a bibliography: "How inclusive shall it be?" No uniform attempt was made to assess the relative importance of references; some entries have apt titles and inconsequential substance, while some excellent material is unobtrusive. I have done this so that the reader may avoid the pitfall of selecting books with seemingly appropriate titles that have nothing to do with the top. Occasionally a brief statement will follow the citation to indicate the contents more clearly than does the title.

The reader with modest library facilities has been kept in mind; it is probable that many general libraries will have a generous sampling from the bibliography. Following each chapter or section has been given a list of numbers corresponding to entries in the tabulation below. These enumerations should be considered representative rather than comprehensive, although the choice has been influenced in part by my estimate of the merit. Within the text itself, citations relating to the bibliography have been indicated by footnote numbers.

Where possible, the publishing house and date of publication of each book is given, but this relates only to the particular volume available to the writer. Some of the works are known to have been issued at other dates and places. It is inevitable that some important references were not cited. The author will be glad to have them reported.

1. ADRY, J. F. *Dictionnaire des Jeux*. Paris: H. Barbou, 1807. (Good for names of tops.)
2. "Aerial Top." *Scientific American,* Vol. 64 (1891), p. 377.
3. ALLEMAGNE, HENRY RENÉ D'. *Histoire des Jouets*. Paris: Hachette, 1902.
4. ———. *Les Jouets à la World's Fair en 1904 à Saint-Louis (U-S)*. Paris: Chez l'auteur, 1908.
5. ———. *Sports et Jeux d'Address*. Paris: Hachette, 1908.
6. ANDREE, RICHARD. *Ethnographische Parallelen und Vergleiche*. Leipzig: Veit, 1889.
7. ———. "Das Kreiselspielen," *Globus*, Vol. 69 (1896), p. 371.
8. *Annali dell'Instituto di Correspondenza Archaeologic* (1852), Plate Q.
9. ARISKA, YOTARO. *History of Japanese Toys* (in Japanese script). Tokyo: Kensetsusha, 1935.
10. ARNING, EDUARD. *Ethnographische Notizen aus Hawaii, 1883–86; Mitteilungen fuer Voelkerkunde in Hamburg*, Vol. 16; Hamburg: Friederichsen, de Gruyter und Co., 1931.
11. AUBOYER, JEANNINE. *La Vie Publique et Privée dans l'Inde Ancienne*. Vol. 6. Les Jeux et les Jouets. Paris: Press Universitaires de France, 1955.
12. AUFENANGER, HEINRICH. *Anthropos,* Vol. 53 (1958), p. 582. (New Guinea)
13. AYRTON, M. CHAPLIN. *Childlife in Japan*. New York: D. C. Heath, 1901.
14. BAILEY, CAROLYN S. *Tops and Whistles. True Stories of Early American Toys and Children*. New York: Viking, 1937.

15. BALFOUR, EDWARD. *Cyclopaedia of India.* London: Quaritch, 1885. (On the subject of the disc.)

16. BARNARD, J. G. "On the Motion of the Gyroscope, etc., with a brief Analysis of the Top." *American Journal of Education,* Vol. 4 (1857–58), p. 529. (Mathematical.)

17. ———. "The Gyroscope." *Johnson's Universal Encyclopedia.* New York: A. H. Johnson, 1876.

18. BARTON, F. R. "Children's Games in British New Guinea." *Journal of the Anthropological Institute,* Vol. 38 (1908), pp. 259–79.

19. BARUS, C. "A Curve-tracing Top." *Science,* New series, Vol. 4 (1896), pp. 444–46.

20. ———. "Mathematical Theory of the Top." *Science,* Vol. 14 (December 20, 1901).

21. BASIL (ST. BASILIUS). *See* GIET, S.

22. BAYLE-MOUILLARD, ELIZABETH F. *Nouveau Manuel Complet. Jeux de Société.* Paris: Roret, 1846. (Concerns the yo-yo and diavolo.)

23. BEAGLEHOLE, E. and P. "Ethnology of Pukapuka (Cook Island)." *Bernice P. Bishop Museum Bulletin,* No. 150, Honolulu, 1938. (Brief and of minor interest.)

24. BEAMS, J. W. "Rotors Driven by Light-Pressure." *Physical Review,* Vol. 72 (1947), p. 987.

25. BÉART, CH. *Jeux et Jouets de l'Ouest Africain.* Vol. 1. Dakar: IFAN, 1955, pp. 377–86.

26. BECQ DE FOUQUIÈRES, LOUIS. *Les Jeux des Anciens.* Paris: Didier, 1873.

27. BEECKMAN, ISAAC. *Journal tenu par Isaac Beeckman de 1604 à 1634.* 4 vols. La Haye: Nijhoff, 1939.

28. BELEZE, GUILLAUME. *Jeux des Adolescents.* Paris: Hachette, 1879.

29. BENNDORF, OTTO. *Griechischer und Sicilische Vasenbilder.* Berlin: Guttentag, 1877. Plate 320. (Yo-yo.)

30. BENSON, J. K. *Book of Sports and Pastimes.* London: C. Arthur Pearson, 1907.

31. BEST, ELDON. "Maori Games." *Transactions and Proceedings of the New Zealand Institute,* Vol. 34 (1901), pp. 55–58.

32. ———. "Games and Pastimes of the Maori." *Dominion Museum Bulletin,* No. 8. Wellington: Dominion Museum, 1925.

33. BIZET, GEORGES. "Jeux d'Enfants." *II. La Toupie; Pianoforte duet;* 1871.

34. BLOCH, RAYMOND. "Origin of Olympic Games." *Scientific American,* Vol. 219 (1968), p. 84. (Javelin.)

35. BOGAERT, ED.-W. *L'Éffet Gyrostatique.* Paris: Beranger, 1912.

36. BOEHME, FRANZ M. *Deutsche Kinderlied.* Leipzig: Breitkopf und Haertel, 1897. (Teetotums.)

37. BOESCH, HANS. *Kinderleben.* Leipzig: Diederichs, 1900.

38. BOHNENBERGER, JOHANN G. F. VON. "Beschreibung einer Maschine Welche die Gesetze der Umdrehung der Erde um ihr Axe, und der Veraenderung der Lage der Erdaxe zu erlaeutern dient," *Annalen der Physik (L. W. Gilbert, Ed.),* Vol. 60 (1819), pp. 60–71. Also in *Tuebingen Blaetter fuer Naturwissenschaft und Arzenkunde (Edit. Autenrieth & Bohnenberger)* III Bandes, erstes Heft, pp. 72–83.

39. BONNEFONT, GASTON. *Les Jeux et les Recreations.* Paris: Maurice Dreyfous, 1888.

40. AUSUBEL, N. (ed.) *Book of Jewish Knowledge.* New York: Crown, 1964.

41. BOUASSE, H. *Gyroscopes et Projectiles.* Paris: Delagrave, 1923.

42. BRAAMS, C. M. "On the Influence of Friction on the Motion of a Top," *Physica,* Vol. 18 (1952), pp.503–14. (Mathematics of Tippe Top.) Also, "The Symmetrical Top." *Nature,* Vol. 170 (July 5, 1952), p. 31. (Short version of above.)

43. BRADY, JOHN. *Analysis of the Calendar (Clavis Calendaria),* Vol. 1. London: Nichols, Sons & Bentley, 1815.

44. BRAND, JOHN. *Observations on Popular Antiquities.* London: Chatto & Windus, 1877.

45. ———. *Dictionary of Faiths and Folklore.* London: Reeves & Turner, 1905.

46. BROWN, CATHERINE. *Folklore,* Vol. 66 (1945), p. 369. (Minor, but has jingle associated with tops.)

47. BROWN, JOHN P. *The Dervishes.* London: Truebner, 1868.

48. BROWN, J. MACMILLAN. *Maori and Polynesian*. London: Hutchinson, 1907.

49. BRUECHNER, A. "Athenische Hochzeitgeschenke." *Mitteilungen des Koeniglich Deutschen Archaelogischen Institut; Athenische Abteilungen,* Vol. 32 (1907), pp. 79, 94. (Magic wheel.)

50. BUCK, E. O. *Popular Mechanics,* Vol. 60 (December 1933), p. 913. (Table game.)

51. BUTLER, S. E. *School Arts,* Vol. 23 (November 1923), p. 166. (Spinners, juvenile.)

52. BUXTON, L. H. DUDLEY. "Anthropology of Cyprus." *Journal of the Anthropological Institute of Great Britain and Ireland,* Vol. 50 (1920), p. 191. (Buzzer.)

53. BUYTENDIJK, F. J. J. *Wesen und Sinn des Spiels.* Berlin: Kurt Wolff, 1933. (Theory of play; yo-yo.)

54. CALLOIS, ROGER. *Jeux et Sports.* Paris: Gallimard, 1967. (Good guidebook.)

55. CALMETTES, PIERRE. *Les Joujoux.* Paris: Doin, 1924. (Diavolo.)

56. CAMP, EZRA J. Motion of an Unsymmetrical Top. Dissertation. Chicago: University of Chicago, 1935. (Mathematical.)

57. CAMPBELL, LEWIS. *Life of James Clerk Maxwell.* London: Macmillan, 1882.

58. CAMPBELL, ROSEMAE WELLS. *Toys and Gyroscopes.* New York: Thos. Y. Crowell, 1959.

59. CARVER, ROBIN. *Book of Sports.* Boston: Lilly, Wait, Colman and Holden, 1834. (Whip-top.)

60. CATS, JACOB. *Huwelyk (Kinderspiel).* Amsterdam: Cornelis, 1779.

61. CHAMPLIN, JOHN D., AND BOSTWICK, ARTHUR E. *Young Folks Cyclopaedia of Games and Sports.* New York: Henry Holt, 1890, pp. 731–36.

62. "Chicago Top-Spinners." *Life,* Vol. 19 (September 10, 1945), p. 97.

63. CHILDE, V. GORDON. "Rotary Motion." *History of Technology,* Vol. I. Oxford: Clarendon Press, 1954.

64. METCALF, REV. FREDERICK. *Charicles.* London: Longmans Green, 1880. (Brief mention of top in antiquity.)

65. CHINNERY, E. W. P. "Mountain Tribes of the Mandated Territory of New Guinea from Mount Chapman to Mount Hagen." *Man,* Vol. 34 (August 1934). (Minor.)

66. CLARETIE, LEO. *Les Jouets, histoire, fabrication.* Paris: Quantan, 1893.

67. CLARKE, WILLIAM. *Boys' Own Book.* Boston: Munroe & Francis, 1847.

68. CLAY, FELIX. "Philosophy of Boys' Games." *Child Study,* Vol. 4 (1911), pp. 101, 132–41.

69. CLERCQ, FREDERICK S. A. DE, AND SCHMELTZ, J. D. *Ethnographische Beschrijving de West-en noord-kunst van Neder landsch Niew-Guinea.* Leiden: P. M. Trap, 1893.

70. COCK, KAREL DE, AND TIERLINCK, ISADOR. *Kinderspiel und Kinderlust in Zuid-Nederland.* Vol. 5. Gent: Siefer, 1905, pp. 140–216. (Comprehensive.)

71. CODRINGTON, R. H. *The Melanesians; Studies in their Anthropology and Folklore.* Oxford: Clarendon Press, 1891, p. 342.

72. COLLIGNON, MAXIME, AND COUVÉ, LOUIS. *Catalog des Vases Peints; Musée National d'Athens.* Paris: Thorin, 1902. (Classical.)

73. COLLINS, A. FREDERICK. *Boys' Book of Amusements.* New York: D. Appleton, 1927.

74. COLLINS, G. N. "A Primitive Gyroscope in Liberia." *National Geographic,* Vol. 21 (June 1910), p. 531. (Whip-tops).

75. COLWELL, R. C., AND HALL, N. I. "High Speed Tops and Gyroscopes." *Review of Scientific Instruments,* Vol. 6 (1935), pp. 238–41.

76. ———. "High Speed Tops and Gyroscopes." *Science,* Vol. 83 (March 20, 1936), p. 289.

77. COLWELL, R. C., AND FULLMER, L. "Motion of a Spinning Top." *Nature,* Vol. 142 (1938), p. 290.

78. COMENIUS, JOHANN AMOS. *Orbis Sensualium Pictus.* (Ed., Johannes Kuehnel). Leipzig: Julius Klinkhardt, 1910, p. 276.

79. CONTENSU, PIERRE. "Couplage entre frottement de glissement et frottement de pivotment dans la théorie de la toupie." *Symposium Célerina, August 20, 1962;* Berlin: Springer, 1963.

80. *Conversations sur les Jeux de la Jeunesse entre un Père et*

ses Enfants, ou Nouvelle Méthode à Instruire les Enfants,
Newmarket, England, 1814.

81. COPLEY, G. N. "The Symmetrical Spherical Top." *Nature,*
Vol. 170 (July 26, 1952), p. 169. (The Tippe Top.)

82. CORLISS, JOHN J. "Unsymmetrical Tops." *Acta Mathematica,*
Vol. 159 (1932), pp. 423–41. (Mathematical.)

83. CORT, AIMÉ DE. *Vlaamsche Kinderspel uit West Brussel.*
Brussel: Kryn, 1931. (Children's games.)

84. CRABTREE, HAROLD. *Spinning Tops and Gyroscopic Motion.*
London: Longmans, Green, 1909. (Good.)

85. CRAIGIE, W. A. *A New English Dictionary.* Vol. 10, Part 2.
Oxford: Clarendon Press, 1928. (Definitions and citations
for "whirligig.")

86. CRUIKSHANK, GEORGE. *The Corsican Whipping Top in Full
Spin,* April 11, 1814. (Cartoon in the Broadley Collection.)

87. CULIN, STEWART. "Chess and Playing Cards." *Report of National Museum,* Washington, D.C., 1896.

88. ———. *Korean Games.* Philadelphia: University of Pennsylvania, 1895. (Excellent pictures.)

89. ———. "Hawaiian Games." *American Anthropologist.* New
series, Vol. 1 (1899), pp. 221–22.

90. ———. "Games of the North American Indians." Extract
from the *24th Annual Report of the Bureau of American
Ethnology,* Washington, D.C.: Government Printing Office,
1907.

91. CUMING, H. SYER. "On the Whirligig or Top." *Journal of
the British Archaeology Association,* Vol. 30 (1874), pp. 37–
42. (Roman occupation of Britain.)

92. "Curious Tops." *Scientific American,* Vol. 74 (1896), pp. 37–
39. (Good illustrations.)

93. DAIKEN, LESLIE. *Children's Games Throughout the Year.*
London: B. T. Batsford, Ltd., 1949. (Good pictures.)

94. ———. *Children's Toys Throughout the Ages.* London:
Spring Books, 1963. (Minor interest.)

95. DAILEY, H. B. "Electrical Top and Motor." *Scientific American,* Vol. 83 (1900), p. 84.

96. DARBOUX, G. "Sur le mouvement d'un corps pesant de révolution fixé par un point de son axe." *Comptes Rendus*

des Séances de l'Académie des Sciences, Vol. 101 (1850), J-D, pp. 111–19, 199–205. (Mathematical.)

97. DAREMBERG, CHARLES VICTOR. *Dictionnaire des Antiquités Grècques et Romaines.* Paris: Hachette, 1881–1889.

98. DEIMEL, RICHARD F. *Mechanics of the Gyroscope.* New York: Macmillan, 1929, ch. 6, pp. 75–92. (Mathematical.)

99. DELEVOY, ROBERT L. *Brueghel, Historical and Critical Study.* Geneva: Skira, 1959, p. 59 and pl. 56.

100. DEMOULIN, GUSTAVE. *Jouets d'Enfants.* Paris: Hachette, 1884. (Conversational treatment of several tops.)

101. DEPEW, ARTHUR M. *The Cokesbury Game Book.* New York: Abington, 1960, pp. 138–39.

102. DEUBNER, LUDWIG. "Spiel und Spielzug der Griechen." *Die Antike.* Vol. 6 (1930), pp. 162–77.

103. DE VRIES, LEONARD. *Flowers of Delight.* New York: Pantheon, 1965. (Reproduces pages of old books on games.)

104. DEWAR, T. I. "Algebraic Gyrostatic Curves." *Engineering* (London), July 17, 1896, pp. 92–93. (Mathematical.)

105. *Dewsbury, the Official Guide.* Cheltenham: E. J. Burrow, 1967.

106. DILLAYE, FREDERIC. *Les Jeux et la Jeunesse.* Paris: Hachette, 1885, pp. 192–95. (Toupie, sabot.)

107. DOMOGAROV, ARKADII SEMENOVIC. *The Free Movements of the Gyroscope* (in Russian). St. Petersburg: Imperial Academy of Science, 1893. Pages XV–XXVI catalog raisonné, 200 references 1749–1893 (in roman script).

108. DONNELLY, RICHARD J.; HELMS, WILLIAM G.; AND MITCHELL, ELMER D. *Active Games and Contests.* New York: Ronald, 1958, pp. 92–94.

109. DOOLITTLE, JUSTUS. *Social Life of the Chinese,* Vol. 2. New York: Harper & Bros., 1865, p. 280.

110. DROST, JOHANNA WILHEMINA PETRONELLA. *Het Nederlandsch Kinderspel voor de Zieventiende Eeuw.* 's-Gravenhage: Martinus Nijhof, 1914.

111. DUMONT, ALBERT, AND CHAPLAIN, JULES. *Les Céramiques de la Grèce Propre.* Paris: Firmin Didot, 1888, pp. 367–68.

112. EDGE-PARTINGTON, JAMES. *An Album of the Weapons, Tools, Ornaments, etc., of the Natives of the Pacific Islands,* 4 vols. Manchester: J. C. Norberry, 1890–1898.

113. EISGRUBER, ELSA. *Spin, Top, Spin.* New York: Macmillan, 1929. (Juvenile, poems and pictures by E.E.)

114. EPSTEIN, PAUL S. "Bemerkung zur Frage der Quantelung des Kreisels." *Physikalische Zeitschrift,* Vol. 20 (1919), pp. 289–94. (Mathematical.)

115. ESQUIEU, LOUIS. *Les Jeux populaires de l'enfance à Rennes.* Rennes: Caillière, 1890. (Names and children's vocabulary.)

116. ETHRIDGE, R., JR. "Game of Teetotum as Practiced by Certain Queensland Aborigines." *Journal of the Archeological Institute,* Vol. 25 (1896), pp. 259–62.

117. *Every Boy's Book: A Complete Encyclopedia of Sports and Amusements.* London: G. Rutledge, 1858.

118. EYMERY, ALEXIS. *Les jeux de quatre saisons.* Paris: [D. Eymery], 1812.

119. FAIRBANKS, ARTHUR. *Catalog of Greek and Etruscan Vases.* Vol. I. Cambridge, Mass.: Harvard Press, 1928, plate no. 568.

120. FEDERLI, HERMANN. *Zu einigen Benennungen des Kreisels in den romanischeen Sprachen.* Zurich: Juris Verlag, 1966.

121. FERRY, ERVIN S. *Applied Gyrodynamics.* London: Wiley, 1932.

122. FINCK. "Note sur la Toupie." *Nouvelles Annales de Mathématique* (Paris), Vol. 9 (1850), p. 310.

123. FISHER, HARRIET F. "The World's Top Top-Maker," *Yankee,* (December 1968), p. 84. "Rhode Island's Top Top-Spinner." *Ibid.,* p. 186. (Story of Dr. J. W. Wilson.)

124. "Flying Propeller" *Scientific American,* Vol 69 (1893), p. 331. (Aerial top.)

125. FOKKER, A. D. "The Rising Top. Experimental Evidence and Theory." *Physica,* Vol. 8 (1941), pp. 591–96.

126. ———. "Hoepels en tollen." *Archives du Musée Teyler.* Serie 3, Vol. 9, Fascicule 4 (1941), pp. 343–424. (Mathematical.)

127. ———. "The Tracks of Tops' Pegs on the Floor." *Archives du Musée Teyler.* Serie 3, Vol. 10 (1953), pp. 215–20. (Mathematical.)

128. FOLEY, DAN. *Toys through the Ages.* Philadelphia: Clinton, 1962. (Bibliography.)

129. FOUCAULT, JEAN BERNARD LEON. "Sur une nouvelle demon-

stration du mouvement de la terre, fondée sur la fixité du plan de rotation." *Comptes Rendus,* Vol. 35 (1852), pp. 420–27.

130. ———. *Proceedings of the Royal Society, London,* Vol. 7 (1854–55), pp. 571–74. (Award in honor of invention of the gyroscope.)

131. FOURNIER, EDOUARD. *Histoire des jouets et jeux d'enfants.* Paris: E. Dentu, 1889. (Toupie, émigrette, diavolo.)

132. FRANKE, HERMANN. "Ueber die Bewegung rotirender Kreisel." Inaugural-Dissertation, Jena, 1874. (Mathematical.)

133. FRANKLIN, ALFRED. *La Vie privée d'autrefois.* Paris: Plon, Nourrit, 1896, Chapter 5.

134. FRASER, ANTONIA. *History of Toys.* Frankfurt-am-Main: Delacorte, 1966. (Lucid.)

135. ———. *Spielzug.* Oldenburg: Gerhard Stalling, 1966. (Illustration of Vaughn children with tops.)

136. FREEMAN, RUTH AND LARRY. *Cavalcade of Toys.* Watkins Glen, N.Y.: Century House, 1942, p. 116.

137. FREEMAN, G. L. AND R. S. *Yesterday's Toys.* Watkins Glen, N.Y.: Century House, 1962, pp. 60–62.

138. FRIEDERS, M. F. "Liftoff Tool for Longstem Tops." *Popular Mechanics,* Vol. 88 (1947), p. 197. *See also* Vol. 121 (1964), p. 161.

139. FROEHNER, CHRISTIAN E. L. W. *Catalogue de la Collection van Branteghem.* 1892, n. 167, pl. 42.

140. FROMAN, ROBERT. *Baseball-istics.* New York: G. P. Putnam's Sons, 1967.

141. FURNESS, HORACE H. *New Variorum Shakespeare.* Philadelphia: Lippincott, 1901, (*Twelfth Night,* parish top.)

142. FURTWAENGLER, A., AND REICHHOLD, K. *Griechischer Vasenmalerei.* II Series. München: F. Bruckmann, 1905, p. 181.

143. GALLOP, E. G. "On the Rise of a Spinning Top." *Transactions of the Cambridge Philosophical Society,* Vol. 19 (1904), p. 356. (Mathematical.)

144. GARDINER, E. NORMAN. *Athletes of the Ancient World.* Oxford: Clarendon Press, 1930.

145. GARMAN, RAYMOND H. *Games, Pastimes and Amusements.* Chicago: Thompson and Thomas, 1906. (Peg-in-the ring; making several types of tops.)

146. GARNETT, LUCY M. J. *Mysticism and Magic in Turkey*. New York: Scribner's, 1912. (Dervishes.)

147. GARSTANG, JOHN. "Excavations at Jericho." *Annals of Archaeology and Anthropology*, Vol. 21 (1934), p. 99, Plate 19, item 2. (Potter's wheel.)

148. Anon. "An Historical Account and Description of Mr. Serson's Whirling Horizontal Speculum, with Its Use in Navigation." *Gentleman's Magazine*. Vol. 24 (1754), pp. 446–48.

149. GERHARD, EDUARD. *Etruskische Spiegel*, 4. Berlin: Reimer, 1867, plate CCCXXVI. (Magic wheel.)

150. GERINI, G. E. "Siamese Festivals." *Encyclopedia of Religious Ethics*, Vol. 5. New York: Charles Scribner's Sons, 1925.

151. GIET, STANISLAS. *Homelies sur l'Hexaemeron*. Paris: Editions du Cerf, 1949.

152. GOMME, ALICE BERTHA. *Traditional Games of England, Scotland, etc.* New York: Dover Press, 1964. (General.)

153. GOODWIN-AUSTEN, H. (discussion of E. B. Taylor article). *Journal of the Anthropological Institute of Great Britain and Ireland*, Vol. 9 (1879), p. 30. (India.)

154. GORDON, LESLEY. *Peepshow into Paradise*. London: George G. Harrup, 1953, pp. 166–68. (General, interesting.)

155. GOW, A. S. F. "Jynx, Rombos, Rhombus, Turbo." *Journal of Hellenic Studies*, Vol. 54 (1934), pp. 3–8.

156. GRABOWSKY, VON F. "Spiele und Spielzuge bei den Dajaken Suedost-Borneos." *Globus*, Vol. 73 (1896), p. 376.

157. GRAEF, BOTHO. "Das Kabirenheiligtum bei Theben." *Mitteilungen des Koeniglich Deutschen Archaeologischen Institut; Athenische Abteilung*, Vol. 15 (1890), p. 374. (Votive tops.)

158. GRAHAM, GEORGE. *Journal of the Polynesian Society*, Vol. 31 (1932), p. 202. (A chant to start a top.)

159. GRAMMEL, R. *Der Kreisel. Seine Theorie und seine Anwendungen*. Braunschweig: Friederich Vieweg, 1920. (Extensive math.)

160. GRASBERGER, LORENZ. *Erziehung und Unterricht im Klassischen Altertum:* Würzburg, 1864. (Literature citations.)

161. GRAY, ANDREW. *Gyrostatics and Rotational Motion*. London: Macmillan, 1918. (Extensive, good.)

162. GREENHILL, A. G. "Mathematics of the Spinning Top." *Nature,* Vol. 60 (1889), pp. 319–22, 346–49.

163. ———— "Mathematical Theory of the Top." *Science,* Vol. 14 (December 20, 1901), pp. 973–75.

164. ————. "Mathematical Theory of the Top." *Annals of Mathematics,* New Series, Vol. 5 (1903–05), pp. 1–20.

165. ————. "Report on Gyroscopic Theory." *Advisory Committee for Aeronautics, Reports and Memoranda No. 146.* London: H. M. Stationery Office, 1914. Chap. 4, p. 81; 5, p. 116; 6, p. 158.

166. GRIAULE, M. "Jeux Dogons." *Travaux et Memoires de l'Institute d'Éthnologie,* 32, Paris, 1938.

167. GRIFFIS, W. E. "Games and Sports of Japanese Children." *Transactions of the Asiatic Society of Japan,* Vol. 2 (1874), pp. 140–58. Also in *Mikado's Empire* by William Elliott Griffis. New York: Harper & Bros., 1900.

168. GRIFFITHS, JOHN. *Paintings in the Buddhist Temples of Ajanta.* Vol. 1. London: W. Griggs, 1896–97, plate 31, p. 30.

169. GRIMSEHL, E., AND TOMASCHEK, R. *Textbook of Physics, Vol. 1 (Mechanics).* London: Blackie & Son, 1932, pp. 157–65. (Discussion leading to Gyro.)

170. GRIOLI, GIUSEPPE. "On the Theory of Asymmetric Gyros." *Symposium Celerina.* Aug. 20–23, 1962; p. 29. Berlin-Goettingen-Heidelburg: Springer, 1963. (Mathematical.)

171. GRISE, JEHAN DE (illustrator for "Roman d'Alexander"). Collotype facsimile of MS Bodley 264. Oxford: Clarendon Press, 1933. (Medieval scene of whipping top.)

172. GROOS, KARL. *The Play of Man.* New York: Appleton, 1901.

173. GRUNWALD, M. "The Top Among Jews and Gentiles." *Edoth* (Jerusalem) Vol. 1 (1946). English summary p. 127. (Teetotum.)

174. GUTS MUTHS, JOHANN C. F. *Spiele zuer Uebing und Erholung des Koerpers und des Geistes.* Hof: Grau, 1878. (Games.)

175. "Gyrograph or Artistic Top." *Scientific American,* Vol. 73 (1895), p. 248. (Compare Barus.)

176. HADDON, A. C. *Study of Man.* New York: G. P. Putnam's Sons, 1898.

177. ———. *Head Hunters, etc.* London: Methuen, 1901. (Murray Island.)

178. ———. *Reports of University of Cambridge Anthropological Expedition to Torres Strait.* Vol. 4, pp. 314–17, 384–86; Vol. 6, pp. 12–15.

179. HALL, KATHERINE S. *Children at Play in Many Lands.* New York: Missionary Education Movement of the U.S. and Canada, 1912.

180. HAMBRUCH, PAUL. *Nauru (Suedsee Expedition 1908–1910),* Vol. 2, B 1, p. 342. Hamburg: L. Friedrichsen & Co., 1913. (South Pacific.)

181. HAMILTON, A. *Maori Art.* Wellington, N.Z.: New Zealand Institute, 1896.

182. HAMILTON, E. I. *St. Nicholas;* Vol. 59 (October 1932), p. 643. (Cardboard disc spinner.)

183. HAMILTON, SIR WILLIAM. *Collection of Engravings from Vases, etc.* Volume 3, Plate Q. Berlin: Tischbein, 1791–1795.

184. HARCOURT-SMITH, CECIL. "Whip Tops." *Hellenic Studies,* Vol. 49 (1929), pp. 217–19.

185. HARTMANN, MARTIN. *Der Islamische Orient,* Band III, p. 14. Leipzig: Rudolph Haupt, 1910. (Dervishes.)

186. HARTWIG, PAUL. *Meisterschalen,* plates XXII, XXVII. Stuttgart: W. Spemann, 1893.

187. HARQUEVAUX, L., AND PELLETIER, L. *200 Jeux d'Enfants.* Paris: Libraire Larousse, 1893. (Toton, bilboquet, whip tops; a table game like skittles.)

188. HAWKESWORTH, JOHN, *An Account of the Voyages Undertaken by Order of His Recent Majesty for Discoveries in the Southern Hemisphere,* Vol. 2. London: Strahan & Cadell, 1773, Chap. II, p. 319. (New Zealand.)

189. HEMBERT, J., AND NIVOIX, P. *Le Diabolo pour tous.* Paris: Duruy et Cie, 1908. (An excellent exposition on the diavolo.)

190. HERCIK, EMANUEL. *Folk Toys; Les Jouets Populaires.* Prague: Orbis, 1951.

191. HERMANN, PAUL. *Denkmaeler der Alterthums.* München:

F. Bruckmann, 1904–1931, Series 1, p. 7, Vol. 2, Tafel 2, plate Aries and Aphrodite. (Magic wheel.)

192. HERVEY, D. F. A. "Malay Games"; *Journal of the Anthropological Institute of Great Britain and Ireland*, Vol. 33 (1903), p. 291.

193. HETZER, HILDEGARD. *Spiel und Spielzug*. Lindau-Bodensee: Verlag Kleine Kinder, 1935. (Preface.)

194. HEWSON, J. B. *History of the Practice of Navigation*. Glasgow: Brown, Son & Ferguson, 1951. (Serson.)

195. HEYDEMANN, H. *Vasensammlungen des Museo Nazionale zu Neapel*. Berlin: Georg Reimer, 1872.

196. HILLIER, MARY. *Pageant of Toys*. New York: Taplinger, 1966. (Good illustration Victorian tops.)

197. HILLS, JEANETTE. *Das Kinderspielbild von Pieter Bruegel*. Wien: Oesterreichische Museum, 1957.

198. HIRN, YRJO. *Les Jeux d'enfants*. Paris: Stock, 1926.

199. HOLMES, REV. J. H. "Introductory Notes on the Toys and Games of the Elema, Papuan Gulf." *Journal of the Anthropological Institute of Great Britain and Ireland*, Vol. 38 (1908), p. 281.

200. HOKE, HELEN, AND PELS, WALTER. *First Book of Toys*. New York: Franklin Watts, 1957.

201. HONE, WILLIAM. *Every Day Book and Table Book*. London: Tegg, 1838, Vol. 1, pp. 199, 253. (Medieval church.)

202. HOORN, GERARDUS VAN. *De Vita Atque Cultu Puerorum Monumentis Antiquis Explanto*. Amsterdam: J. H. DeBussy, 1909. (Classical.)

203. HOPKINS, G. M. "Electrical Top." *Popular Science Review* (1879), p. 211.

204. HUGENHOLTZ, N. M. "On Tops Rising by Friction." *Physica*, Vol. 18 (1952), pp. 515–27. (Mathematics of Tippe Top.)

205. HUNT, SARAH E. *Games and Sports the World Round*, 3rd Ed. New York: Ronald Press, 1964. (Maori, Eskimo.)

206. HURGRONJE, C. S. *The Achenese*, Vol. 2. Leyden: E. J. Brill, 1906, p. 190.

207. JACKSON, EMILY. *Toys of Other Days*. London: Country Life, 1908.

208. JACOBS, J. A. "Note on the Behavior of a Certain Sym-

metrical Top." *American Journal of Physics,* Vol. 20 (1952), p. 517. (Tippe Top.)

209. JAHN, OTTO. "Ein Vasenbild der Muenchener Sammlung." *Berichte verhandlunger koenig. Saechsischer Gesellschaft der Wissenschaft zu Leipzig,* Vol. 6 (1854), p. 256. (Magic wheel.)

210. ———. "Denkmaeler und Forschungen," *Archaelogische Zeitung;* Jahrgang XV, No. 108 (December 1857), pp. 106–9 and Tafel CVIII. (Spinner.)

211. JAKOB, FRIEDERICH AUGUST L. *Deutschland's Spielender Jugend.* Leipzig: Kumer, 1883. (Dancing snake.)

212. (Japanese Encyclopedia) *Daihyakka jitan,* Vol. 10. Tokyo: Yashburo, 1934. Vol. 11, Tokyo: Heibonsha, 1954.

213. JELLETT, JOHN H. *Theory of Friction.* London: Macmillan, 1872, pp. 181–87. (Mathematical analysis.)

214. J.J. (PROBABLY J. JORDAN). "Les Toupies." *La Nature* (Dec. 14, 1895), 24ème Année, No. 1176. (Note, this is source of reference 92. Excellent.)

215. JOHNSON, WALTER R. "Description of an Apparatus Called the Rotoscope, for Exhibiting Several Phenomena and Illustrating Certain Laws of Rotary Motion." *American Journal of Science and Arts,* Vol. 21 (1832), pp. 265–80.

216. JOLY, RENÉ. *Jouets et Jeux d'Antan.* Paris: Sociète Nouvelle des Éditions Bias, 1947.

217. JONQIÈRES, J. P. E. "Au sujet de certaines circonstances qui se presentent dans le mouvement de la toupie." *Comptes Rendus,* Vol. 102 (1886), p. 1519. (Mathematical.)

218. JOYA, MOCK. *Things Japanese.* Tokyo: Tokyo News Service Ltd., 1958. (General.)

219. JUD, J., AND JABERG, K. *Sprach- und Sachatlas Italiens und der Sudschweiz.* Zofingen (Schweiz) Ringier & Co., 1928–1940, Band IV, Karte 751.

220. KATE, H. TEN. "Beitrage zur Ethnographie der Timorgruppe." *Internationales Archiv fuer Ethnographie,* Vol. 7 (1894), p. 242.

221. KAUDERN, WALTER. *Games and Dances in Celebes.* Ethnographical Studies in Celebes, Vol. 4. Goeteborg: Elanders Boktryckeri, 1925–44. (Excellent.)

222. KELLER, OTTO. *Die Antike Tierwelt,* Vol. 2. Leipzig: W. Engelmann, 1913. (Magic wheel.)

223. KERN, O. "Die Boiotischen Kabiren." *Hermes,* Vol. 25 (1890), p. 5. (Much like Winnefeld.)

224. KETTELKAMP, LARRY. *Spinning Tops.* New York: Morrow, 1966. (Lucid.)

225. KINGSTON ACADEMY. *Book of Games Practiced at the Kingston Academy.* Philadelphia: Benjamin Warner, 1821. (Kingston Academy's location indefinite, but probably near London. Text is juvenile, but illustrations may be source of some Daiken figures.)

226. KIPP, CHAS. T. "An Old Form of Top Revived." *School Science and Mathematics,* Vol. 20 (1920), p. 113. (Supported-top.)

227. KIRK, H. C. "The Truth About the Gyroscope." *Popular Astronomy,* Vol. 19 (1911), p. 209.

228. KLEIN, ANITA. *Child Life.* New York: Columbia University, 1932, plate XVIII.

229. KLEIN, FELIX. *Mathematical Theory of the Top.* New York: Scribner's, 1897.

230. KLEIN, F., AND SUMMERFELD, A. *Ueber die Theorie des Kreisels.* Leipzig: Teubner, 1897. (Extensive, mathematical.)

231. KOHL, J. A. *Kitsche-Gami,* Vol. I. Bremen: Scheunemann, 1859, p. 119. (Letter tells of seed and stones used as tops by North American Indians.)

232. LABORDE, E. D. *Harrow School.* London: Winchester Publications, 1948. (Amusements included tops.)

233. LAFFARGUE, J. "La Toupie magneto-electrique." *La Nature* (August 25, 1890), p. 176.

234. LANE, EDWARD W. *Customs and Manners of Modern Egypt.* London: J. Murray, 1860, p. 433. (Dervish.)

235. LANGLOTZ, ERNST. *Griechische Vasen in Wurtzburg.* Muenchen: J. B. Obernetter, 1932, p. 147 and Tafel 238.

236. LANSDALE, HENRY. *The Worthies of Cumberland.* London: Rutledge, 1875, (Troughton.)

237. LEMKE, ELIZABETH. "Uraltes Kinderspielzug." *Zeitschrift des Vereins fuer Volkskunde* (1895), p. 185. (Names, classical.)

238. LEVEZOW, KONRAD. *Antiken Denkmaeler in Antiquarium des Koeniglicher Museums zu Berlin; Galerie der Vasen.* Berlin: Koenigliche Akademie der Wissenschaften, 1834.

239. LOEWE, HEINRICH. "Trendel," *Juedisches Lexikon.* Berlin: Juedischer Verlag, 1927–1930.

240. "Lift-Off Tool for Holding Long-Stem Top." *Popular Mechanics,* Vol. 121 (April 1964), p. 161.

241. LORENZ, H. "Kurtze Abteilung der Bewegungs-gleichungen-des Kreisels." *Physikalische Zeitschrift,* Vol. 20 (1919), pp. 294–96. (Mathematical.)

242. LUIKEN, JOANNES. *Des Menschen Begin, Midden, en Einde.* Leiden: A. W. Sijthoff, 1881. (Peg-top, whip-top.)

243. LUKACH OR LUKE, HARRY CHARLES. *City of Dancing Dervishes.* London: Macmillan, 1914.

244. MCCLEES, HELEN. *Daily Life of the Greeks and Romans.* New York: Metropolitan Museum of Art, 1924. (Figure of woman spinning whip-top.)

245. MCCLINTOCK, INEZ AND MARSHALL. *Toys in America.* Washington: Public Affairs Press, 1961. (History, commerce.)

246. MACLAGEN, ROBERT CRAIG. *Games and Diversions of Argyleshire.* London: David Nutt, 1901.

247. MACMILLAN, W. A. *Dynamics of Rigid Bodies.* New York: McGraw-Hill, 1936, pp. 243–49, 329–31, 451–53. (Mathematical.)

248. *Malaysia Official Year Book,* Vol. 4 (1964). Kuala Lumpur: Government Press, 1966, pp. 561–62.

249. MARQUARDT, JOACHIM. *Das Privatleben der Roemer.* Leipzig: Hirzel, 1886.

250. MARRAN, RAY J. *Games Outdoors.* New York: Thos. Y. Crowell, 1940, pp. 81–84.

251. ———. *Playthings for Indoor and Outdoor Fun.* New York: Appleton-Century, 1940, pp. 104–17, 138–39.

252. MASON, BERNARD S., AND MITCHELL, ELMER D. *Theory of Play.* New York: Ronald Press, 1935, pp. 87–88. (Explanation of contests.)

253. MAXWELL, J. C. "On a Dynamical Top, for exhibiting the phenomena of the motion of a system of invariable form about a fixed point, with some suggestions as to the Earth's

motion." *Transactions of the Royal Society, Edinburgh,* Vol. 21, pp. 559–70. (Mathematical.)

254. ———. *Scientific Papers of James Clerk Maxwell, edited by W. P. Niven.* Cambridge: University Press, 1890. (Part I, p. 127, deals with color-top.)

255. MILANI, LUIGI A. *Monumenti Scelti R. Museo Archaeologico di Firenze,* Tavel IV. Firenze: Bencini, 1905.

256. MILLINGEN, JAMES. *Peintures Antiques de Vases Grecques.* Rome: Romans, 1813, plate 45. (Magic wheel.)

257. MITZKA, WALTHER. *Deutscher Wortatlas.* Vol. 1. Karte Kreisel. Giessen: Wilhelm Schmitz, 1951. (Extraordinary word list for the top in the German language.)

258. MORISON, SAMUEL ELIOT. *Admiral of the Ocean Sea.* Boston: Little, Brown, 1942, pp. 361–62. (Columbus.)

259. NARES, ROBERT. *Glossary "Parish Top."* London: Reeves & Turner, 1888.

260. NEEDHAM, JOHN. *Science and Civilization in China,* Vol. 4. Cambridge: University Press, 1965, plate 278. (Helicopter top.)

261. NESTEROFF, DMITRI. "Whirling Dervishes Still Gyrating after Thirteen Centuries." *Beirut Daily Star* (September 7, 1968).

262. NEWBERRY, JOHN. *See* THWAITE, M. F.

263. NEWBERRY, R. J. "Some Games and Pastimes of Southern Nigeria." *The Nigerian Field,* Vol. 7 (July 1938), pp. 131–33.

264. NISHIZAWA, TEKIHO. *"Japanese Toys"* (in Japanese script). Tokyo: Yuzanaku, 1965.

265. "Novel Top." *Scientific American,* Vol. 67 (1892), p. 5. (Air-propelled.)

266. NUGENT, M. *St. Nicholas,* Vol. 29 (1902), p. 428. (Juvenile; momentum imparted by tops.)

267. OLSON, O. E. *Popular Science,* Vol. 144 (January 1944), p. 138. (Juvenile; board game.)

268. "Organize a Top-Spinning Contest." *Recreation,* Vol. 48 (March 1955), p. 134.

269. PAGE, LEIGH. *Introduction to Theoretical Physics.* New York: D. Van Nostrand, 1952, pp. 157–66. (Mathematical treatment of top or gyroscope.)

270. PANOFKA, T. *Annali dell'Instituto de Correspondenza Archaeologico* (1852), p. 322, plate Q. (Magic wheel.)

271. PAULY, A. F. VON. *Real-Encyclopaedie.* Stuttgart: Metzler, 1948. (Name of top.)

272. PERRY, JOHN. *Spinning Tops.* London: Sheldon Press, 1929. (Extensive, excellent.)

273. Persius Flaccus. Satires, III, 50. Translation and commentary by John Conington. Oxford: Clarendon Press, 1893. (Persius Flaccus about A.D. 34–62.)

274. PERSON, C.-C. "Disposition de l'appareil de Bohnenberger pour les differents latitudes." *Comptes Rendus,* Vol. 35 (1852), pp. 5449–5542.

275. ———. "L'appareil de Bohnenberger pour la precession des equinoxes peut servir à constater la rotation de la terre." *Ibid.,* pp. 417–20.

276. PETERS, MONTE. "Main Gasing [Top Spinning]"; *The Straits Times Annual* (1956), pp. 68–71; Singapore. (Malaysia tops and spinning; good.)

277. PETRIE, W. M. F. *Kahun, Gurob, and Hawara.* London: Kegan Paul, Trench, Truebner, 1890. (Whip-tops.)

278. ———. *Social Life in Ancient Egypt.* London: Constable, 1923.

279. ———. *Objects of Daily Use; British School of Archaeology in Egypt.* London: Quarich, 1927.

280. PLANCK, MAX. "Zur Quantelung des asymmetrischen Kreisels." *Setzungsberichte der Preussischen Akademie der Wissenschaft,* Vol. 33 (1918), pp. 1116–74. (Mathematical.)

281. PLISKIN, W. A. "The Tippe Top." *American Journal of Physics,* Vol. 22 (1954), pp. 28–32. (Mathematical.)

282. PLUECKER. "Ueber der Fessel'schemachine." *Annalen der Physik und Chemie,* Band XC (1853), pp. 174, 348, 628. (Early gyroscope.)

283. POINSOT, M. *Theorie nouvelle de la rotation des corps.* Paris: Bachelier, 1851. (Mathematical.)

284. POMA DE AYALA, FELIPE HUAMAN. "Nueva Coronica y Buen Gobierno." *(Codex peruvien illustre);* Travaux et Mémoires de l'Institut d'Ethnologie, 23. Paris, 1936.

285. PRELLER, LUDWIG. *Berichte Saechsische Gesellschaft Wissenschaft,* Vol. 4 (1852), pp. 89–92, Tafel V, VI. (Classical yo-yo.)

286. ———. *Archaeologischer Zeitung,* Vol. XI (1853), p. 312. (Yo-yo.)

287. RABECQ-MAILLARD, M. M. "Jeux et jouets d'autrefois." *Institute Pédagogique(France National),* Expo. December 12, 1961–March 10, 1962. (Citations of tops in art.)

288. RAUSCH, HEINRICH A. "Das Spielverzeichnis im 'Geschict-Klitterung' *Gargantua." Dissertation Kaiser Wilhelm Universitaet zu Strassburg.* Strassburg: J. H. Ed. Heitz, 1908.

289. RECHE, OTTO. *Kaiserin-Augusta Fluss; Suedsee Expedition 1908–1910,* Vol. II a 1. Hamburg: L. Friedrichsen & Co., 1913. (New Guinea.)

290. REED, A. H. AND A. W. *An Illustrated Encyclopedia of Maori Life.* Wellington, N.Z.: A. H. and A. W. Reed, 1963.

291. REED, CHARLES H. "Stone Spinning Tops from Torres Strait, New Guinea." *Journal of the Anthropological Institute of Great Britain and Ireland,* Vol. 17 (1887), pp. 85–90.

292. ———. "An Account of a Collection of Ethnological Specimens Formed During Vancouver's Voyage in the Pacific Ocean, 1790–95." *Journal of the Anthropological Institute of Great Britain and Ireland,* Vol. 21 (1891), p. 107.

293. REICHE, F. "Zur Quantelung des asymmetrischen Kreisels." *Physikalische Zeitschrift,* Vol. 19 (1918), pp. 394–401. (Mathematical.)

294. REMISE, JAC. *Golden Age of Toys.* Lausanne: Edita Lausanne, 1967. (Clown top.)

295. RICHTER, G. M. A., AND HALL, L. F. *Red-figured Athenian Vases in the Metropolitan Museum of Art.* New Haven: Yale University Press, 1936, p. 103, fig. 74. (Yo-yo.)

296. RIPLEY, G. S. *Book of Games.* New York: Association Press, 1954. (Top-spinning contests.)

297. ROCHHOLZ, ERNST L. *Allemanische Kinderlied.* Leipzig: J. J. Weber, 1857, pp. 419–420. (Names for tops and games.)

298. ROMERO, EMILIA. *Juegos del antiguo Peru.* Mexico City: Ediciones Llama, 1943.

299. ROTH, HENRY LING. *Natives of Sarawak and British North Borneo,* Vol. I. New York. Truslove & Comba, 1896, pp. 103, 104, 367.

300. ROTH, WALTER E. "Introductory Study of the Arts, Crafts and Customs of the Guiana Indians," *U.S. Bureau of American Ethnology, 38th Annual Report, 1916–17.* Washington, D.C.: Government Printing Office, 1924. (Humming top; seed.)

301. ROUTH, E. J. *Dynamics of a System of Rigid Bodies,* 4th ed. London: Macmillan, 1884, pp. 111–122. (Mathematical treatment of top's motions.)

302. *Saint Petersburg Compte Rendu de la Commission Archaeologique,* 1863, Plate V. (Magic wheel.)

303. SAKAMOTO, KAZUYA. *Japanese Toys.* Rutland, Vt.: Charles E. Tuttle, 1965. (Essentially same as entry 316, with minor variations in text and photographs. Good pictures.)

304. SANG, EDWARD. Remarks on the gyroscope in relation to his "Suggestion of a new Experiment which would demonstrate the Rotation of the Earth" read before the Society, 24 March 1856; *Transactions of the Royal Scottish Society of Arts,* Vol. 4 (1856), pp. 413–20. (Sang read paper of above content on 3 March 1836 but did not publish.)

305. *Saturday Review* (London), Vol. 58 (1884), p. 33. (Written by a non-top-spinner and quite disdainful.)

306. SCHEIBLE, JOHANN. "Die Gute Alte Zeit." *Das Kloster,* Band 6; Stuttgart: 1845–49. (Children's games, including whip-top.)

307. SCHLIEMANN, HEINRICH. *Ilios, City and Country of the Trojans.* New York: Harper & Bros., 1880. (Terra-cotta top and whorls.)

308. SHEPPARD, HAJI MUBIN. *Malaysian Tops.* Forthcoming publication.

309. SHORT, JAMES. "An Account of an Horizontal Top; Invented by Mr. Serson." *Philosophical Transactions,* Vol. 47 (1752), pp. 352–53.

310. SIEVEKING, JOHANNES. "Nackter Mann mit Kreisel." *Die Bronze der Sammlung Loeb,* p. 66, Figure 27. (Etruscan style whip-top.)

311. SKEAT, W. W. *Malay Magic.* New York: Barnes & Noble, 1966, p. 485.

312. SMITH, A. "Note on the Theory of the Spinning Top." *Cambridge Mathematical Journal,* Vol. 1 (1846), pp. 47–48.

313. SMITH, CECIL H. *Catalog of Vases in the British Museum,* Vol. 3. London: British Museum, 1896, pp. 366–367. (Magic wheel; see also Dumont and Chaplain.)

314. SNELL, E. S. "The Rotoscope." *Annual Report, Smithsonian Institution, 1885,* Washington, D.C.: Smithsonian Institute, p. 157. (Type of gyroscope; *see also* JOHNSON, W. R.)

315. SOLIS-COHEN, EMILY, JR. *Hanukkah.* Philadelphia: Jewish Publication Society of America, 1937. (Puppet play, *The Magic Top,* with Mary Garson as co-author.)

316. SONOBE, KIYOSHI (photos), AND SAKAMOTO, KAZUYA (text). *Japanese Toys.* Rutland, Vt.: Tuttle, 1965. (Excellent presentation.)

317. SPINNA (PSEUD). *Fifty New Tricks for all Kinds of Looped String Tops.* London: Gordon Press, 1932. (Yo-yo.)

318. STAMKART, F. J. "Ueber die Bewegung eines Kreisel um seine Spitze." *Annalen Physik und Chemie,* Vol. 91 (1854), pp. 462–81. (Mathematical.)

319. STARR, FREDERICK. "Japanese Toys and Toy-Collectors." *Transactions of the Asiatic Society of Japan, 2nd series,* Vol. 3 (December 1926), pp. 101–16. (Disappointing—". . . tops, we but mention them.")

320. STEELE, J. L. "Top Topics." *Outing,* Vol. 40 (May 1902), pp. 231–34. (Newsy discussion.)

321. STELLA, JACQUES. *Les Jeux et Plaisirs d'Enfance.* Paris: C. Stella, 1657. (Period art includes peg-top and whip-top spinning.)

322. STEPONAITIS, V. *Lietuviu Iiaudies Zaidimai ir Pramogos (Lithuanian Folk Toys and Pastimes).* Valstybine Vilnius, 1956.

323. STEWARD, JULIAN H. (ED.). "Handbook of South American Indians," *Bureau of American Ethnology, Bulletin 143.* Washington, D.C.: Government Printing Office, 1949. Robert H. Lowie, "The Northwestern and Central Ge," Vol. 1,

p. 506; John H. Rowe, "Inca Culture at the Time of the Spanish Conquest," Vol. 2, p. 277; Alfred Metraux, "Tribes of the Eastern Slopes of the Andes," Vol. 3, p. 501; David B. Stout, "The Choco," Vol. 4, p. 274; "Games and Gambling," Vol. 5, pp. 505, 510.

324. STIRLING, EDWARD C. "Report of Work on Horne Scientific Expedition to Central Australia. Part IV." *Anthropology*. London: Dulau, 1896, p. 86.

325. STRUTT, JOSEPH. *Sports and Pastimes of the People of England*. London: Methuen & Co., 1903.

326. "Support; Handle to Hold Top." *Popular Mechanics*, Vol. 73 (June 1940), p. 929.

327. SUTTON-SMITH, BRIAN. *Games of New Zealand Children*. Folklore Studies 12. Berkeley: University of California Press, 1959.

328. SYNGE, J. L. "On a Case of Instability Produced by Rotation." *Philosophical Magazine*, Vol. 43 (1952), pp. 724–28. (Mathematical.)

329. SWINBURNE, J. "How a Top Stands Up." *Scientific American Supplement* 80 (September 25, 1915), p. 197. (Greenfield adds comment.)

330. TALCOTT, LUCY. "Vases and Kalos-names from an Agora Well." *Hesperia*, Vol. 5 (1936), p. 333.

331. TAYLOR, EVA G., AND RICHEY, M. W. *The Geometrical Seaman*. Cambridge: Hollis & Carter, 1962. (Discusses John Serson.)

332. TAYLOR, RICHARD. *Te Ika A Maui, or New Zealand and its Inhabitants*. London: Wertheim & Macintosh, 1885.

333. TELLKAMP, HERMANN. "Versuch zur Begruendung einer moeglichst einfachen Theorie und Erklarung der Kreiselbewegung." *Annalen Physik und Chemie*, Vol. 98 (1856), pp. 558–570. (Mathematical.)

334. THORNDIKE, LYNN. *History of Magic and Experimental Science*, Vol. 1. New York: Macmillan, 1923, ch. 21.

335. THWAITE, M. F. *A Facsimile Reproduction of a Little Pretty Pocketbook, Printed for John Newberry London 1767*. Introduced by M. F. Thwaite. New York: Harcourt, Brace & World, 1967.

336. TIPPETT, JAMES S. *Toys and Toy Makers*. New York: Harper & Bros., 1931. (Color top.)

337. "Top Spinning to Women's Soccer." *Pelita (Singapore)* Vol. 1, No. 7, 3rd Quarter (1963), pp. 7–8. (May be simplified Peters.)

338. TRAORE, MAMADOU. "Jeux et Jouets des Enfants Foula." *Bulletin Institut Français d'Afrique Noire*, Vol. 2 (1940), p. 243.

339. TREGAR, E. "The Maoris of New Zealand." *Journal of the Anthropological Institute of Great Britain and Ireland*, Vol. 19 (1889), p. 115.

340. *Tricks with Yo-yo and Spinning*. Evanston, Ill.: Donald F. Duncan Co., 1962.

341. TUER, ANDREW W. *Pages and Pictures from Forgotten Children's Books*. London: Leadenhall Press, 1898–9. (Interesting prints.)

342. ———. *Forgotten Children's Books*. London: Leadenhall Press, 1898. (Good pictures.)

343. TYLOR, EDWARD B. "History of Games." *Fortnightly Review*, New Series Vol. 25 (1879), pp. 735–47.

344. UHLE, MAX. *Pachacamac (Peruvian Expedition 1896)*. Philadelphia: University of Pennsylvania, 1903.

345. VETT, CARL. *Dervish Diary*. Los Angeles: Knud K. Mogensen, 1953.

346. VRIES. *See* DE VRIES

347. WAGNER, HERMANN. *Illustrierte goldener Kinderbuch*. Leipzig: Otto Spamer, 1888. (Text and pictures.)

348. ———. *Der gelehrte Spielkamerad*. Leipzig: Otto Kamer, 1891. (Toys.)

349. WALKER, G. T. "On a Dynamical Top." *Quarterly Journal of Pure and Applied Mathematics*, Vol. 28 (1896), pp. 175–84.

350. WALTERS, H. B. *Greek and Etruscan Vases in the British Museum*. Oxford: Oxford University Press, 1896, Vol. 4, pl. IX, text F223, pp. 136, 164.(Magic wheel.)

351. WARD, DAVID P. *Diabolo, The Game and its "Tricks."* London: L. Upcott Gill, 1908.

352. WARRING, C. B. "A Curve Tracing Top and a Curious Optical Illusion." *Science,* Vol. 4 (1896), pp. 533–34.

353. WATKINS, FRANCES E. "Hopi Toys." *Museum Leaflet #19.* Los Angeles: The Southwest Museum, 1946.

354. WATZINGER, CARL. *Griechischer Vasen in Tuebingen.* Tuebingen: Reutlingen, Gryphius, 1924. Pl. 25, No. E78.

355. WEHRHAN, KARL. *Kinderspiel: Handbuecher zur Volkskunde,* Vol. 4. Leipzig: Heim, 1909, pp. 63–65.

356. WHITTLE. *Spinning Tops of Naples.* (Fiction; not relevant.)

357. WINNEFELD, H. "Das Kabirenheiligtum bei Theben." *Mitteilungen des Kaiserlich Deutchen Archaeologisch Instituts; Athenisches Mitteilungen.* Vol. 13 (1888), p. 426. (Whip-top.)

358. WOLTERS, PAUL. "Ein Salbegefass aus Tarent." *Muenchener Jahrbuch der Bildenen Kunst,* Vol. 8 (1913), pp. 83–96. (Whip-top shown.)

359. WORTHINGTON, A. M. *Dynamics of Rotation.* London: Longmans, Green, 1897, pp. 154, 159. (Mathematical.)

360. *W.P.A. in New Mexico; The Spanish-American Song and Game Book.* Compiled by workers of the Writers' Program. New York: A. S. Barnes, 1940. (pp. 60–61 pictures.)

361. YAMADA, TOKUHEI. *Toys of Japan* (in Japanese script). Tokyo: Hara-Shoten, 1968.

362. *Youthful Sports.* Philadelphia: Jacob Johnson, 1802. (Scenes of whip-top and peg-top spinning.)

363. "Yo-yo Pronounced a Success at Dalton (New York City) School." *The New York Times,* February 13, 1969, p. 42.

364. *Yo-Yo Secrets.* (Pamphlet of Union Wadding Co., toy manufacturer) by Mister Yo-Yo (Bob Rule). Atlanta: Bob Rule, 1971. (Good illustrated description of play with yo-yo.)

365. Z. DR. "La Toupie Hydraulique." *La Nature* (August 3, 1889), p. 160. (Toy with water chamber creates fountain when spinning.)

366. ———. "Un Nouveau Gyroscope." *La Nature* (March 28, 1891), p. 257. (Toy commonly seen today, with demonstration equipment.)

367. ZINGERLE, IGNAZ V. *Deutsche Kinderspiel im Mittelalter.* Innsbruck: 1873.

269

INDEX

Illustrations are indicated in italics.

Index

Index